ACG Type Portrait

R-18
Characters in the book are all adults.

Pinky girl with pink hair captivates attention wherever she goes, exuding a stunning exterior and confident demeanor that make her stand out effortlessly in a crowd.

However, as you get closer to her, you'll discover another unexpected side. Behind her bold exterior lies a shy and gentle heart.

When faced with strangers or unfamiliar situations, she unconsciously reveals a hint of shyness and timidity, which only adds to her charm and allure.

She possesses not only outward confidence and sophistication but also inner tenderness and warmth.

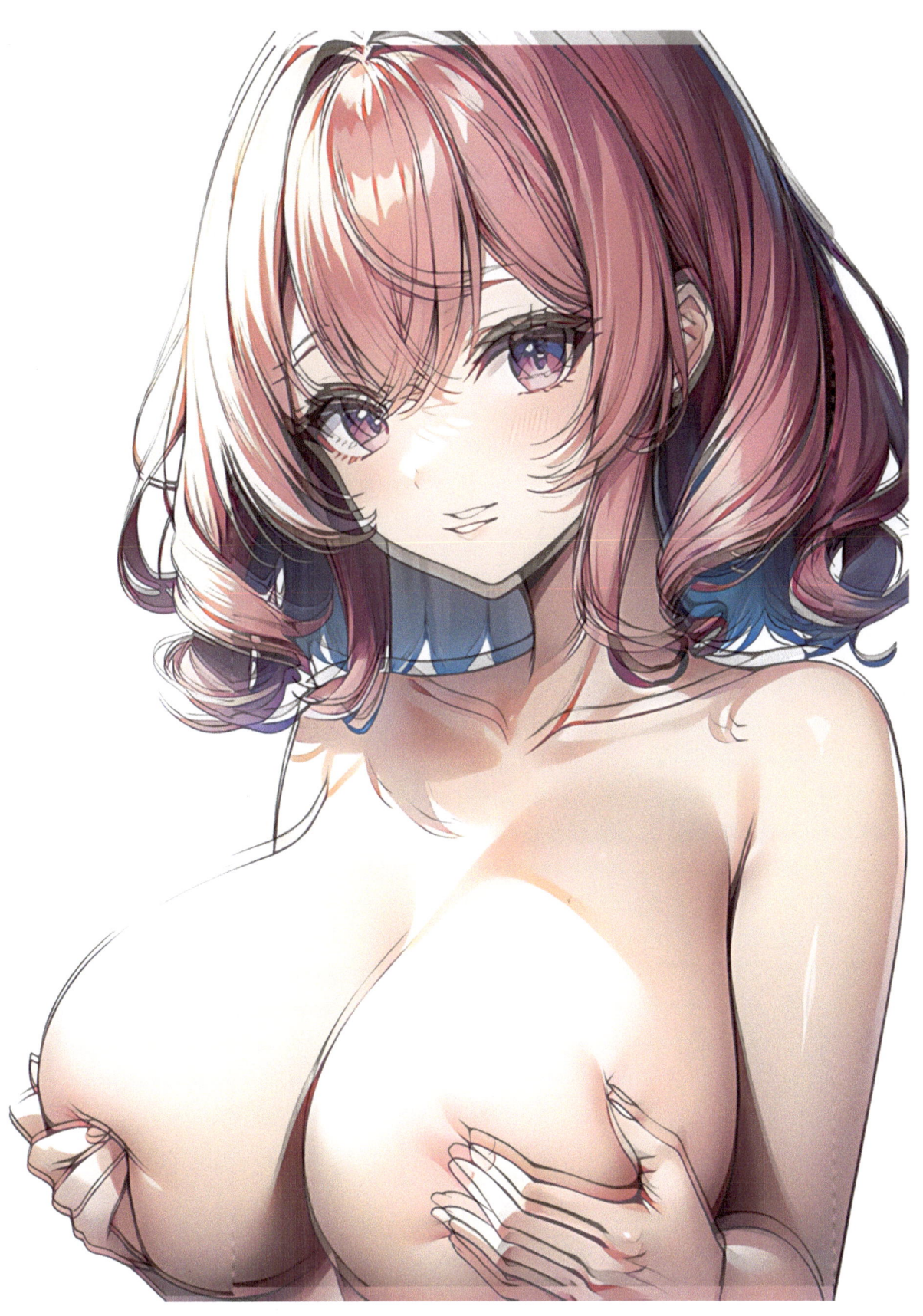

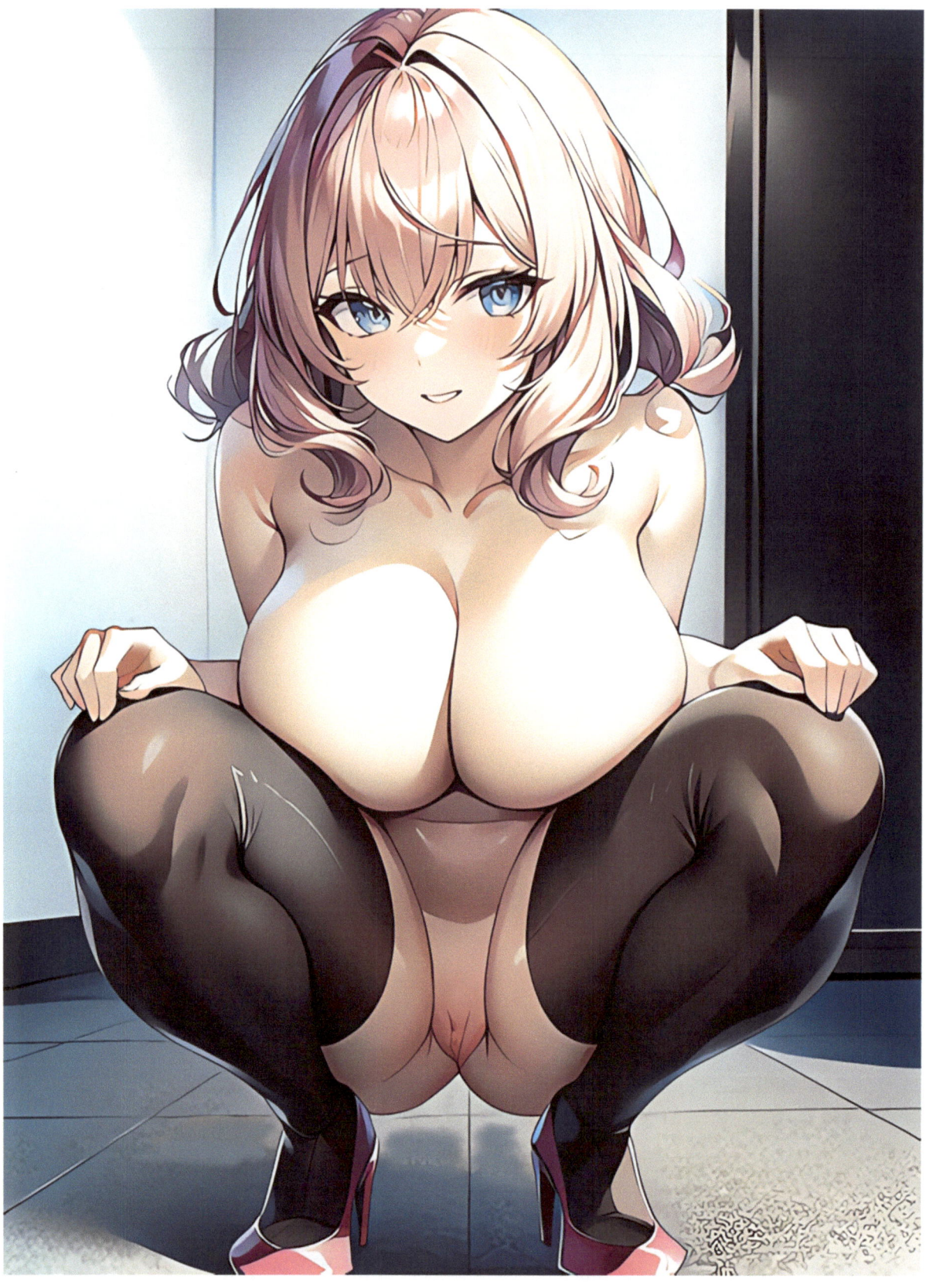

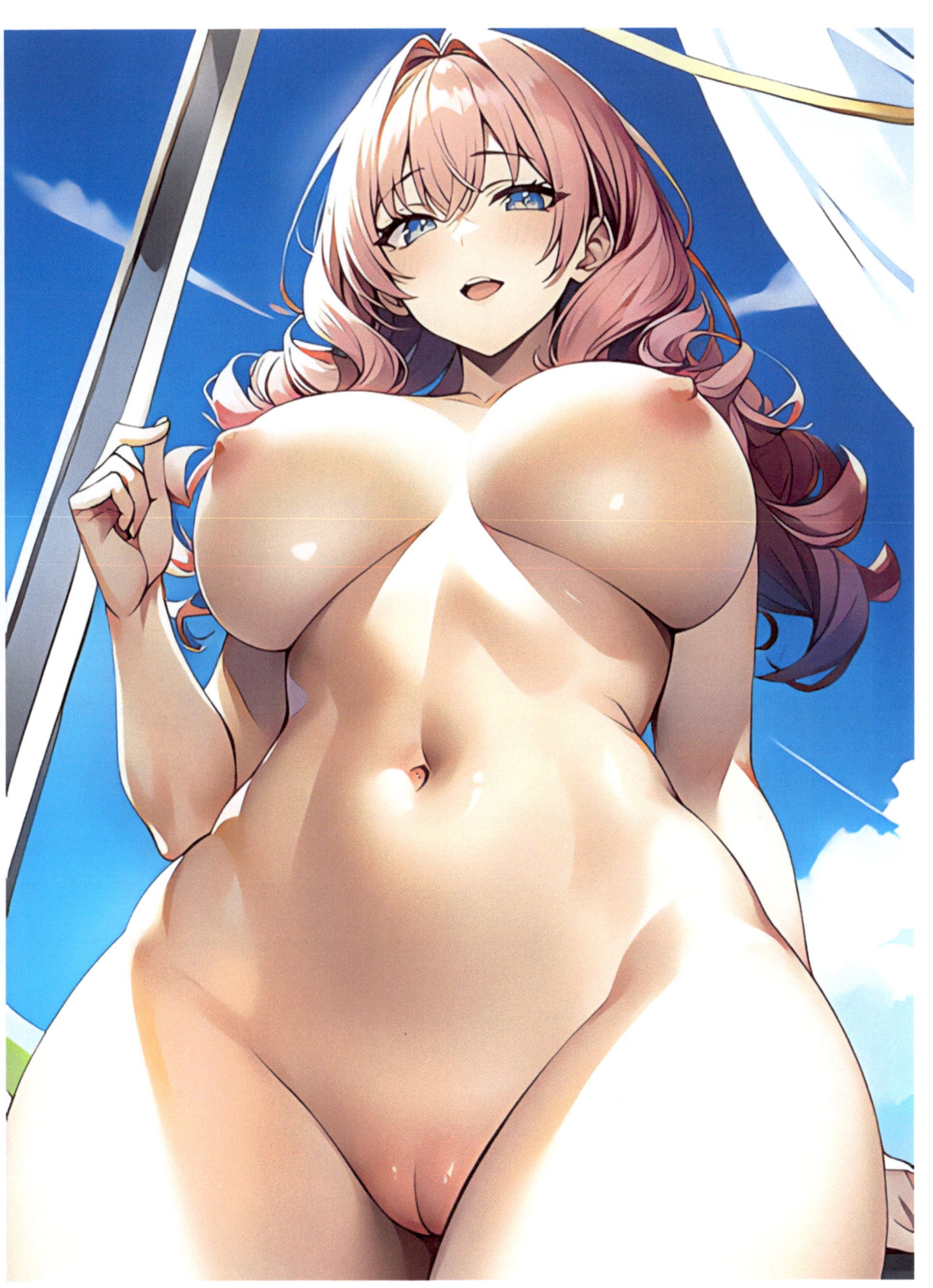

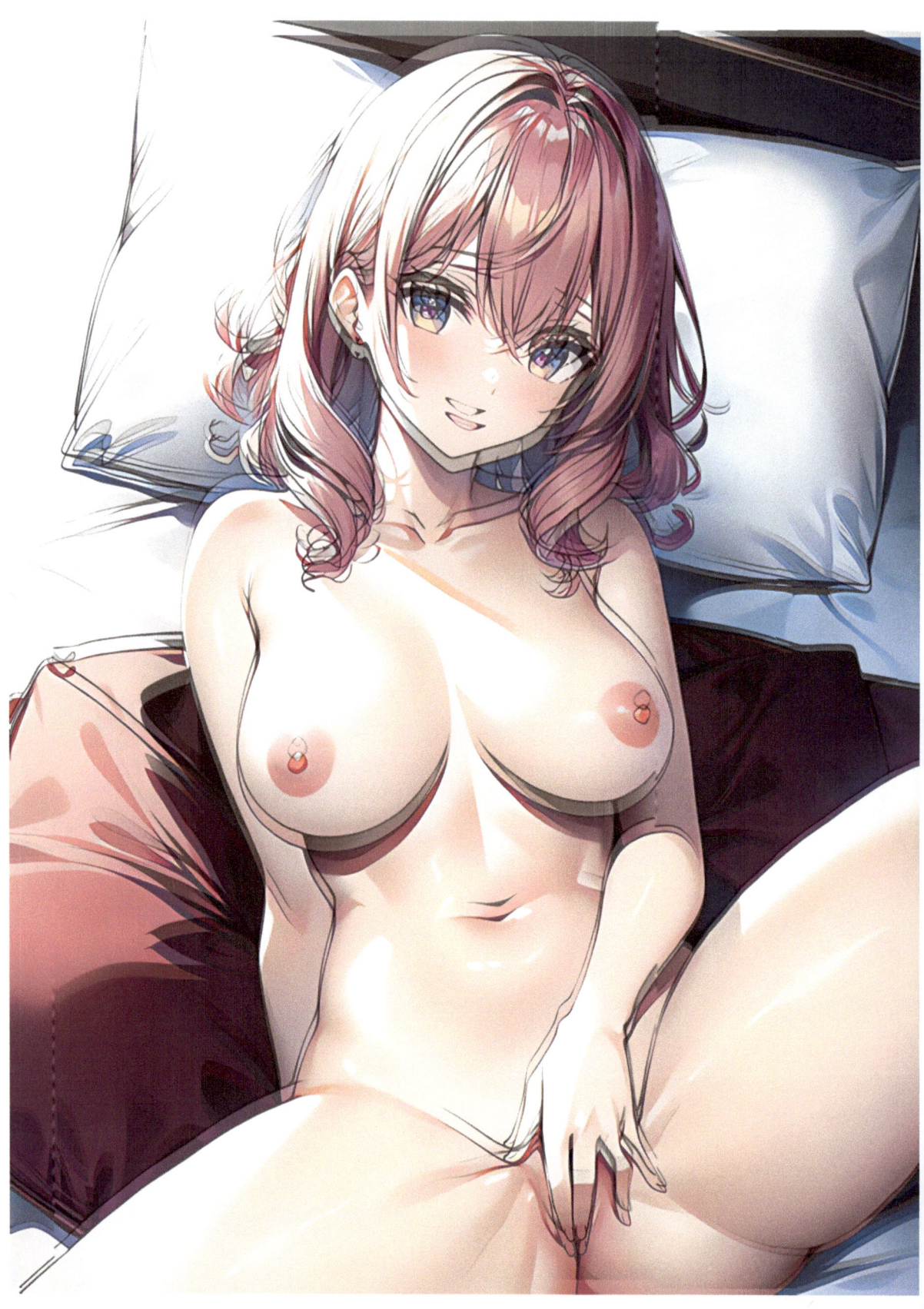

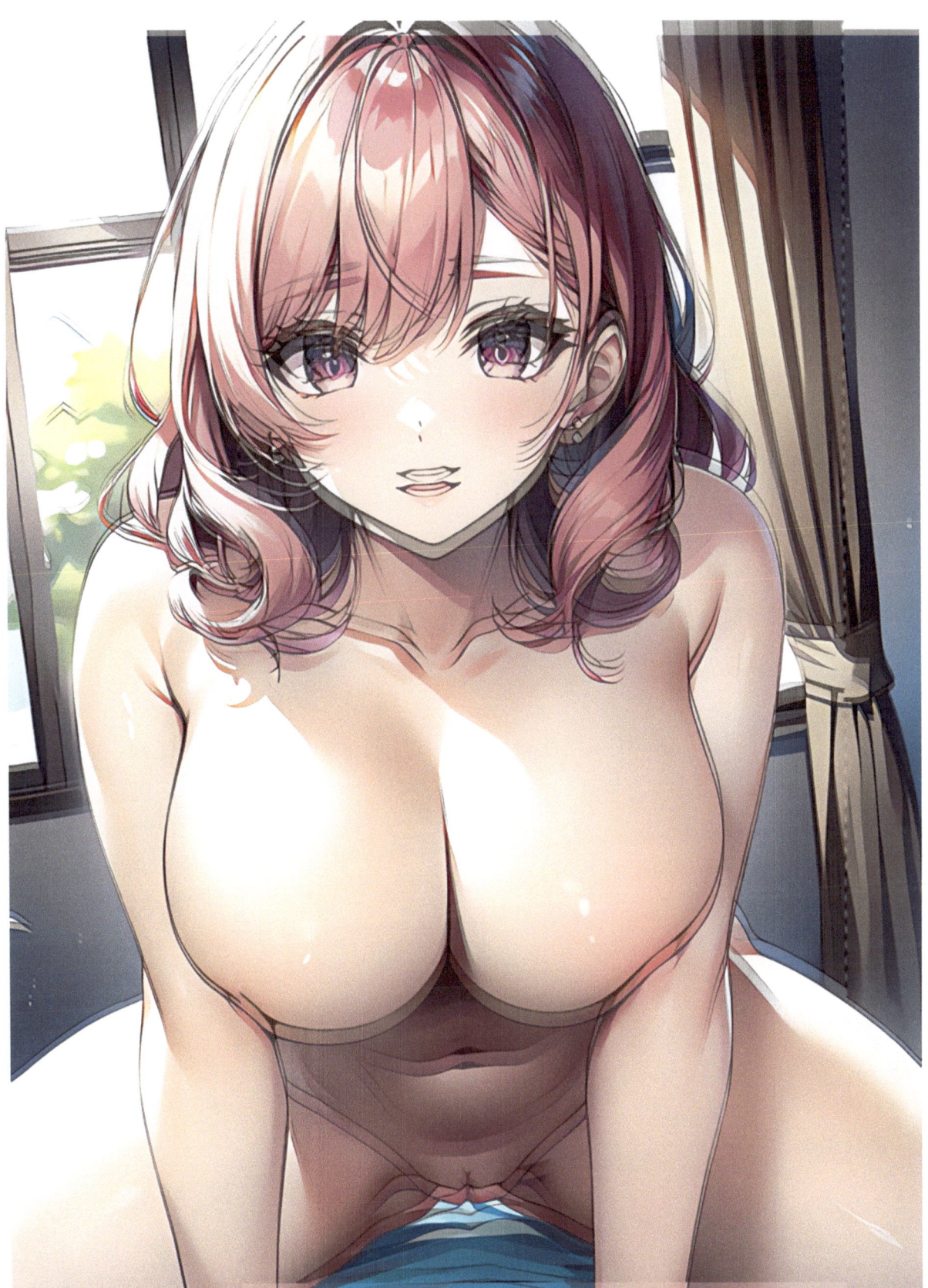

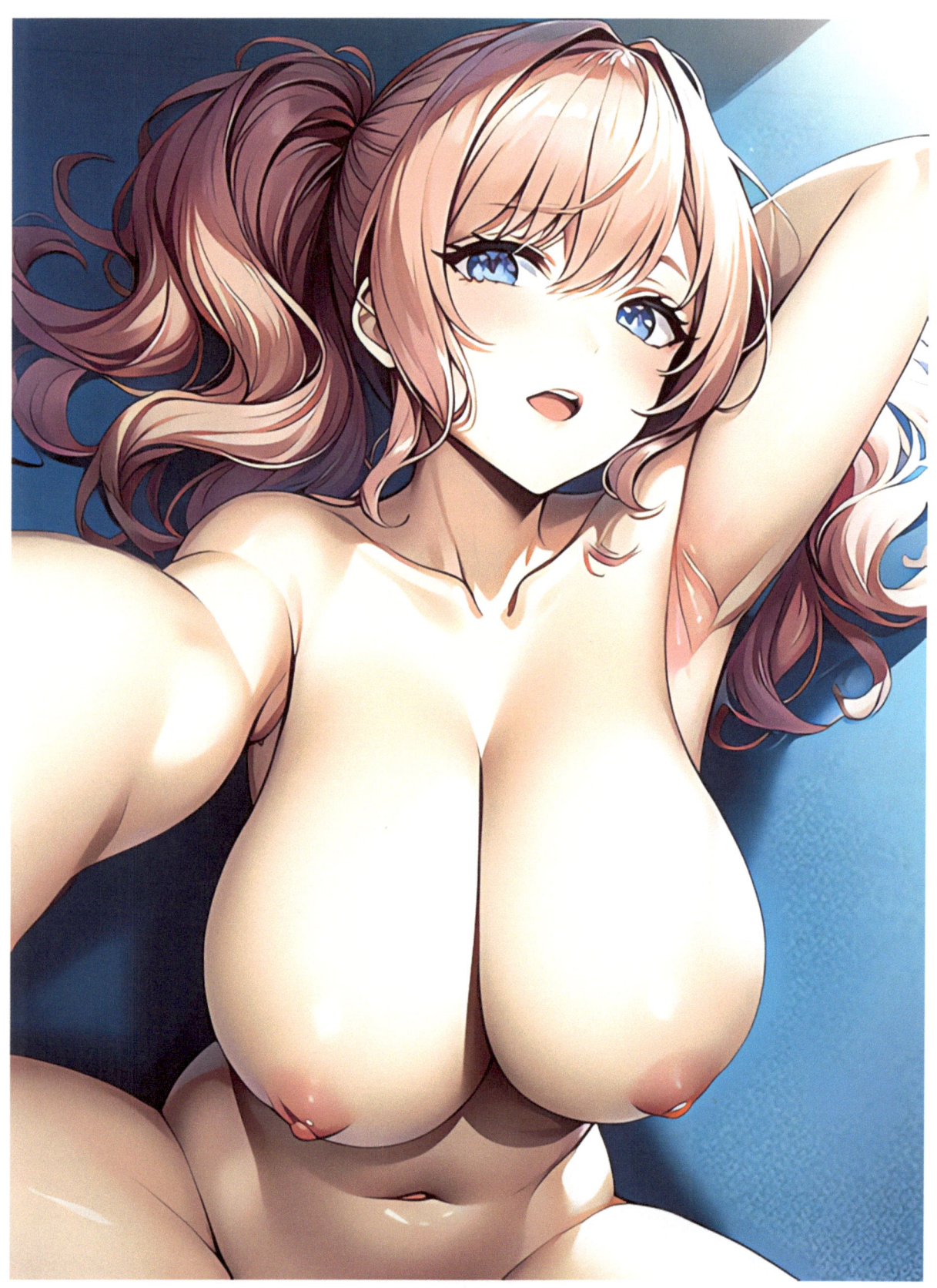

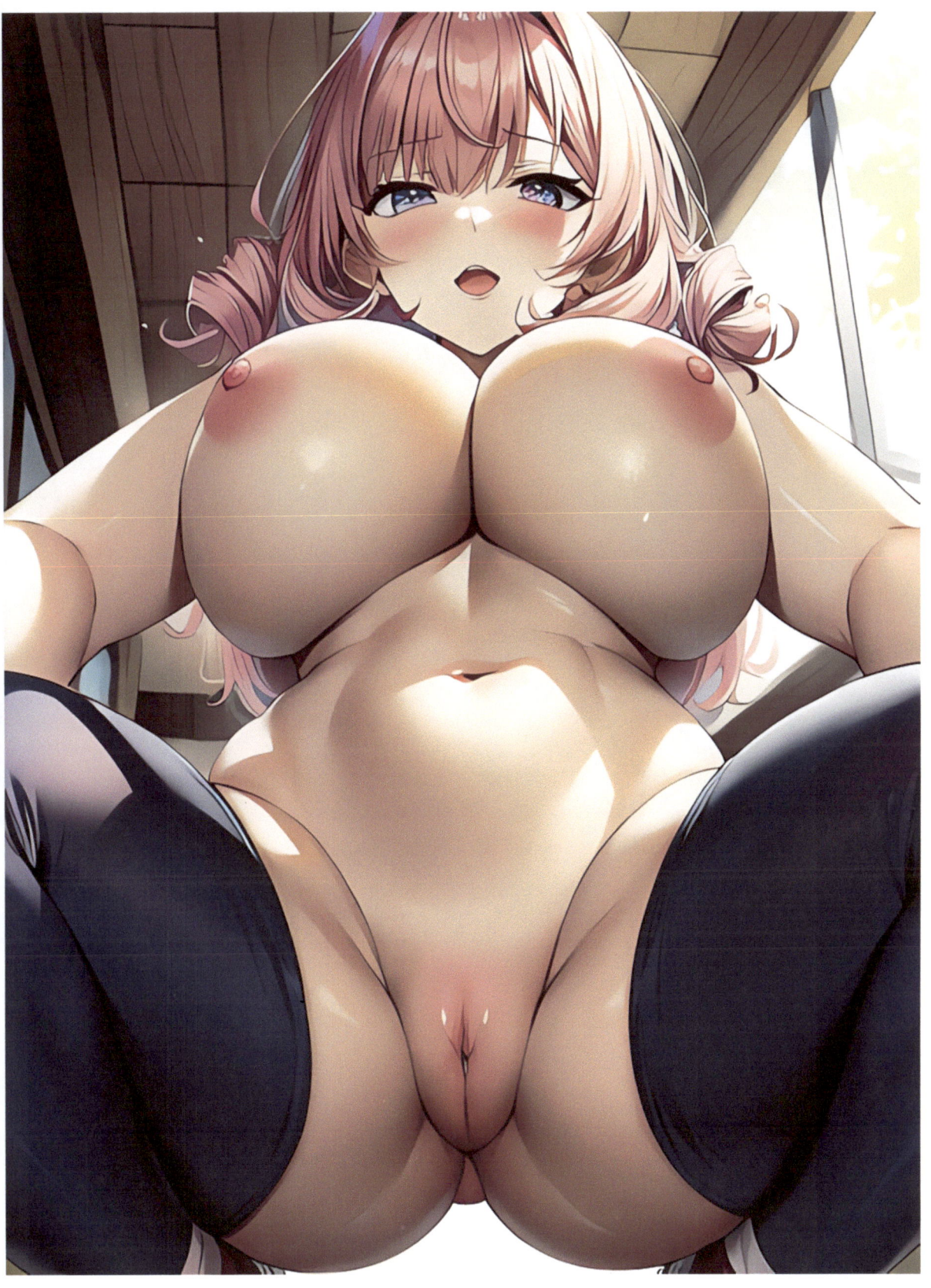

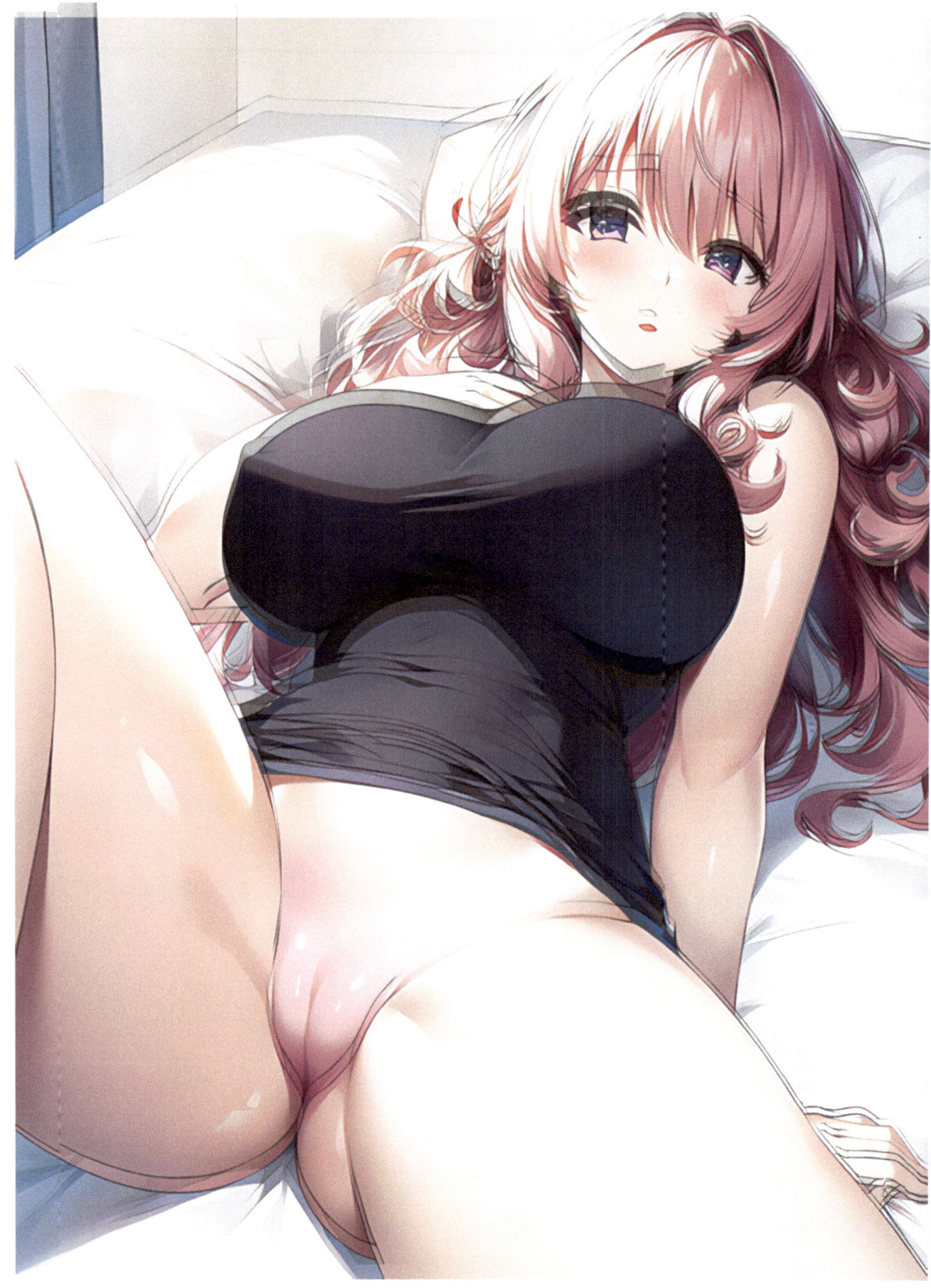

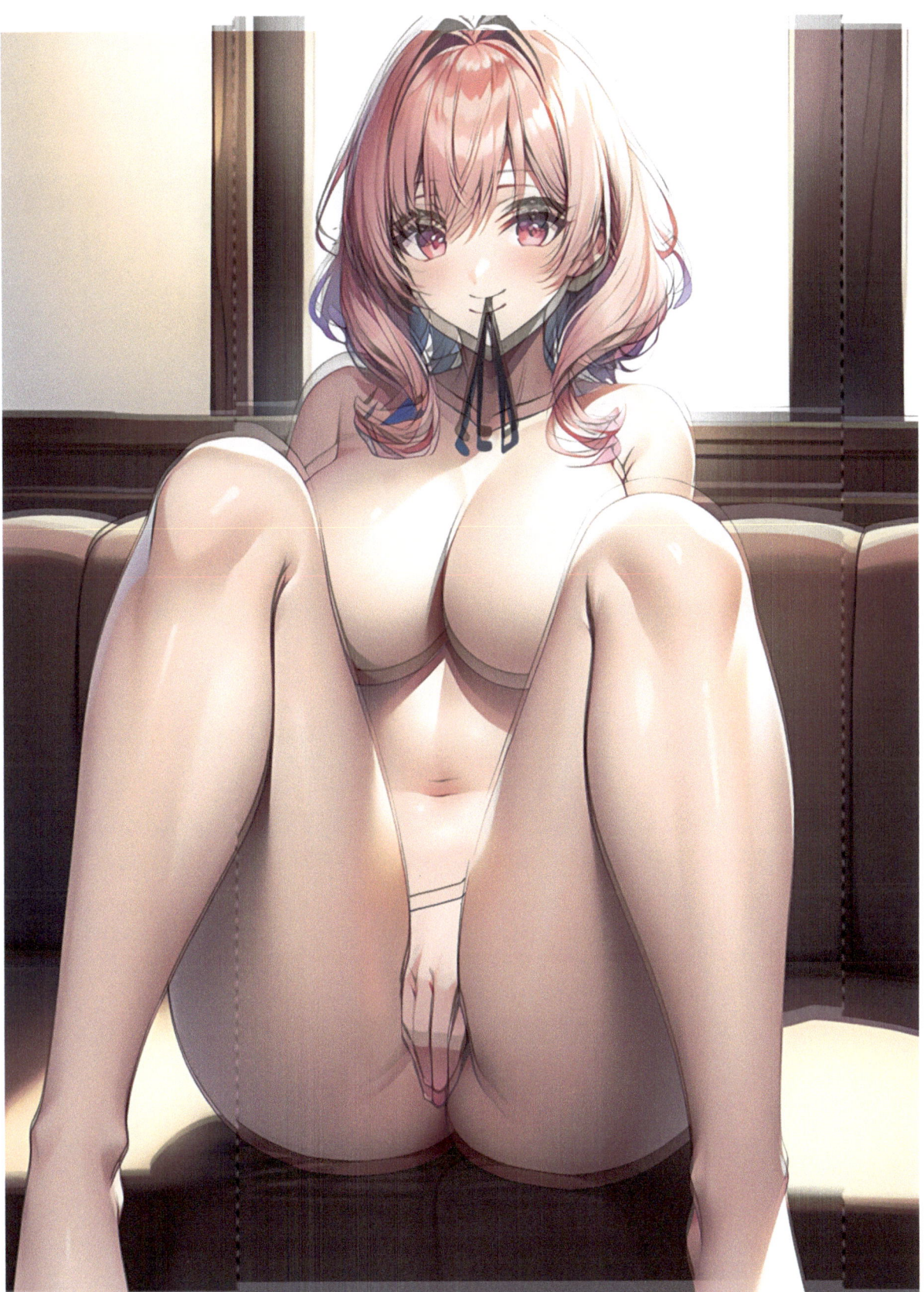

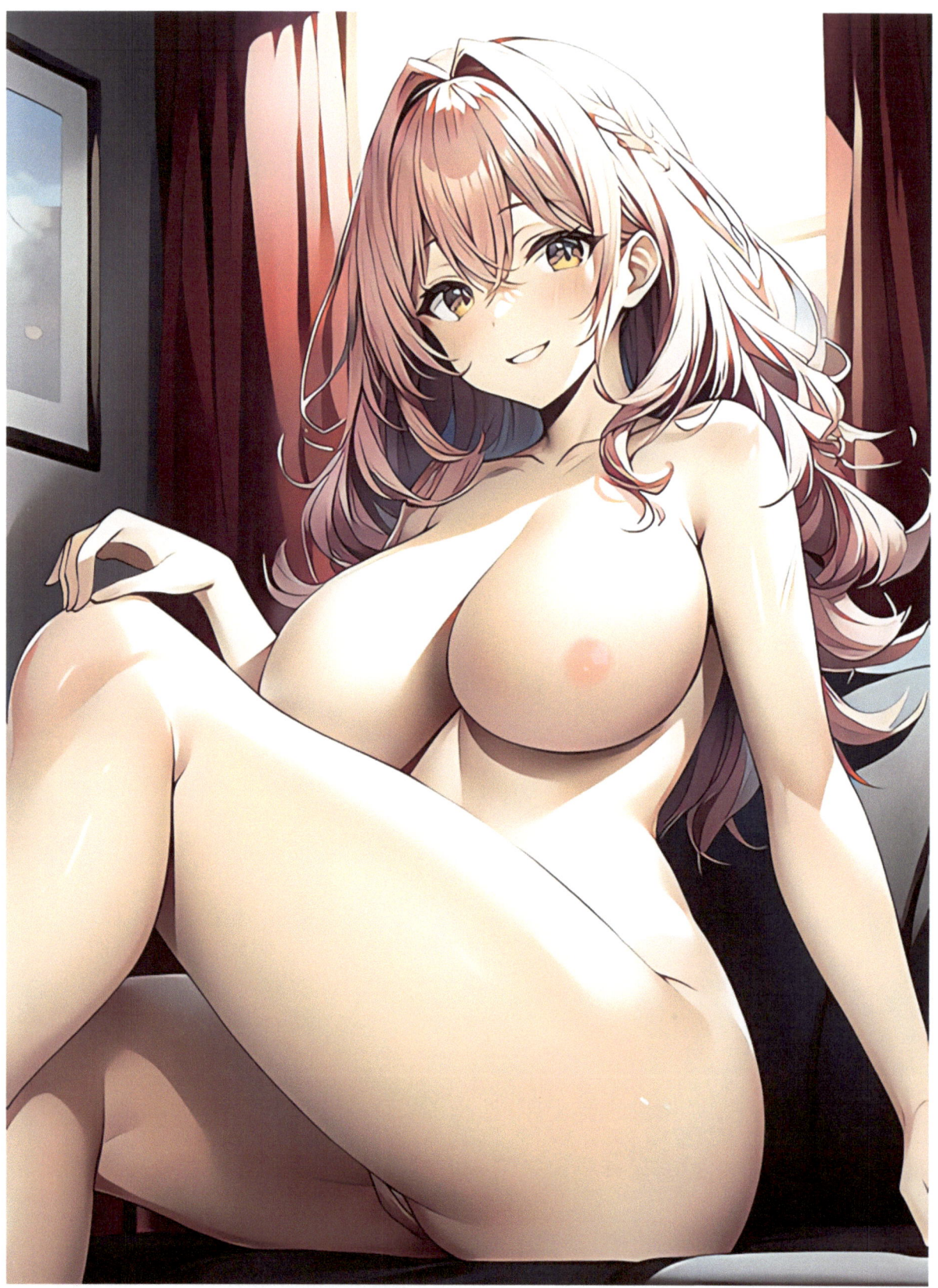

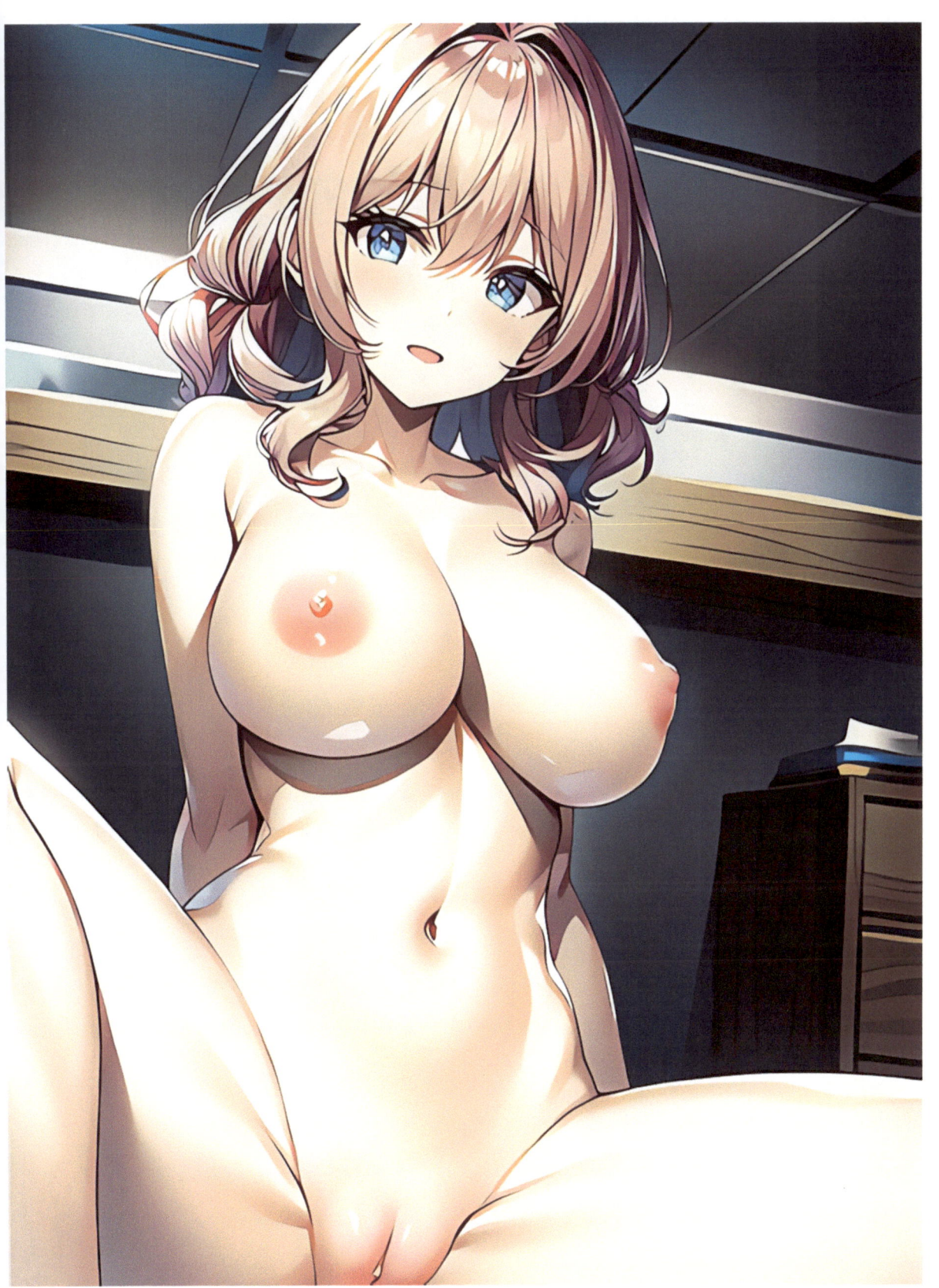

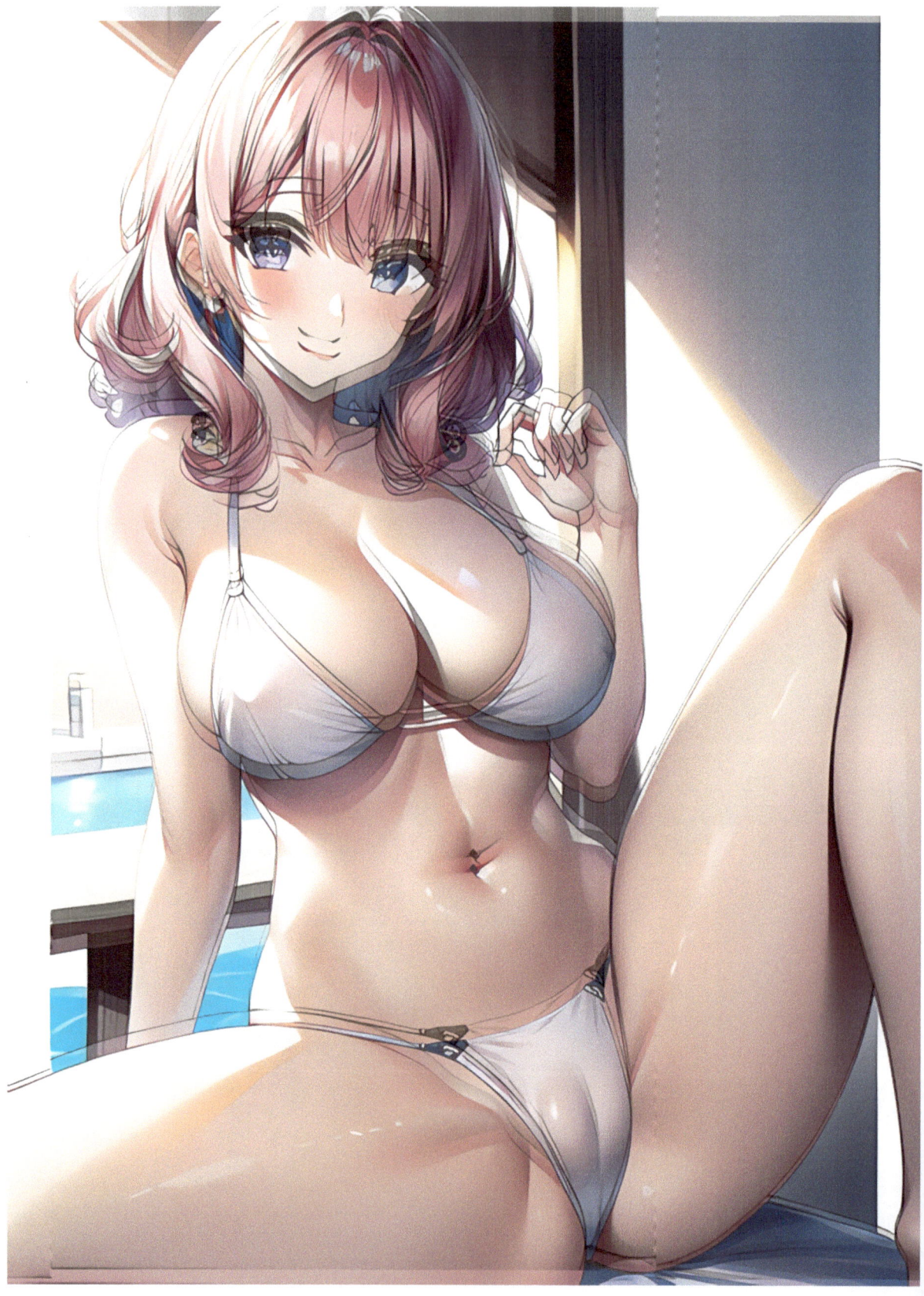

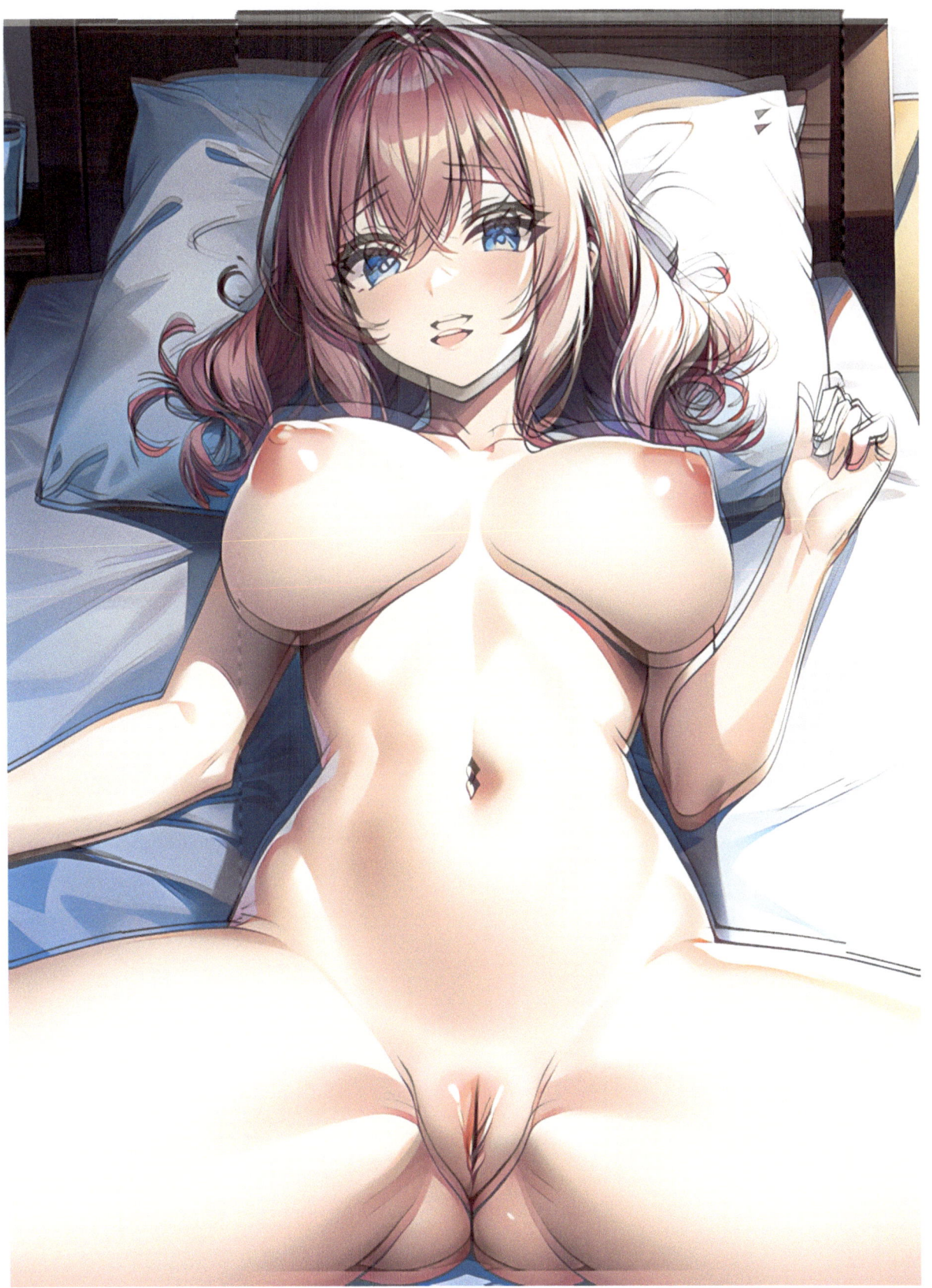

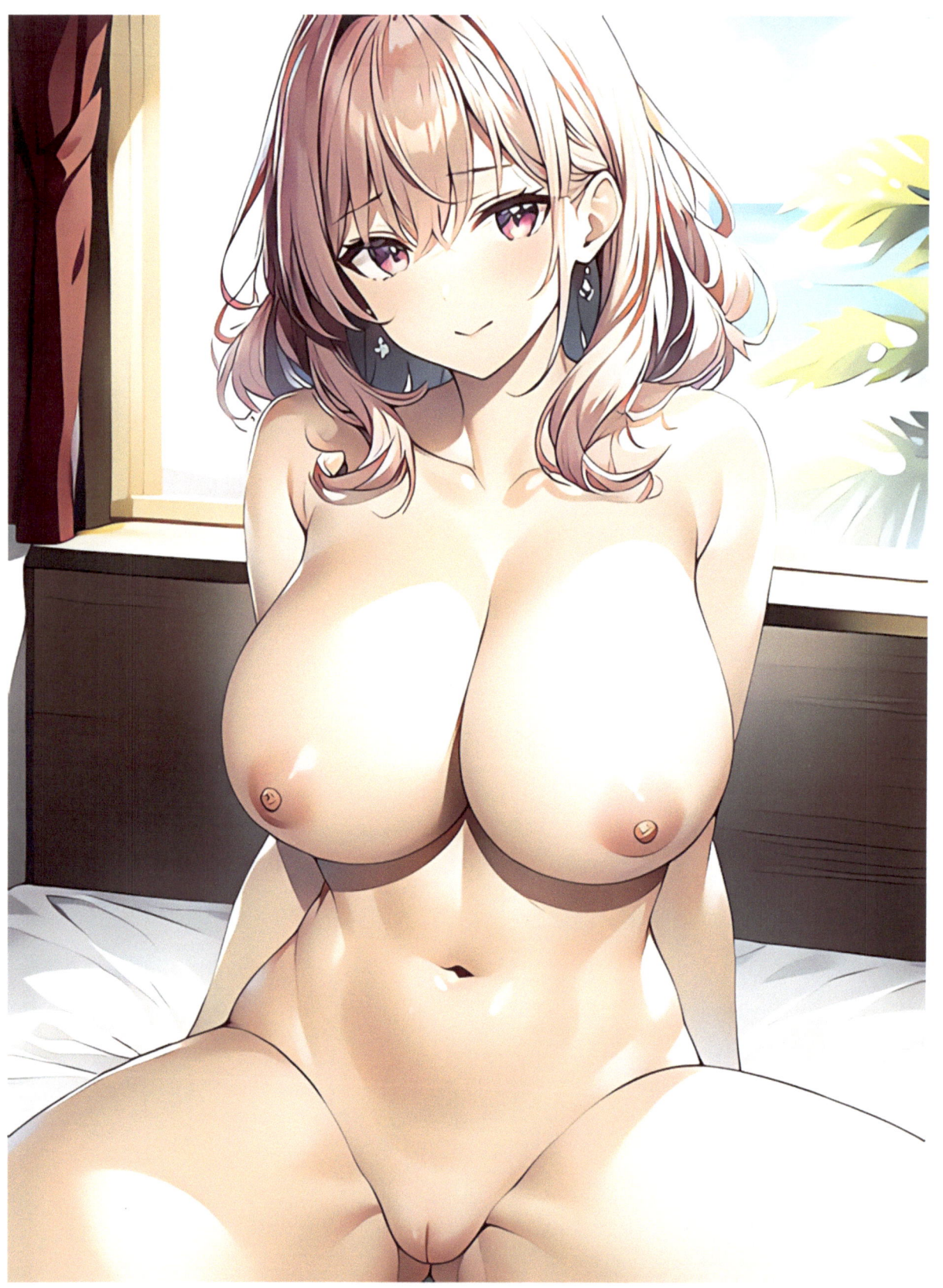

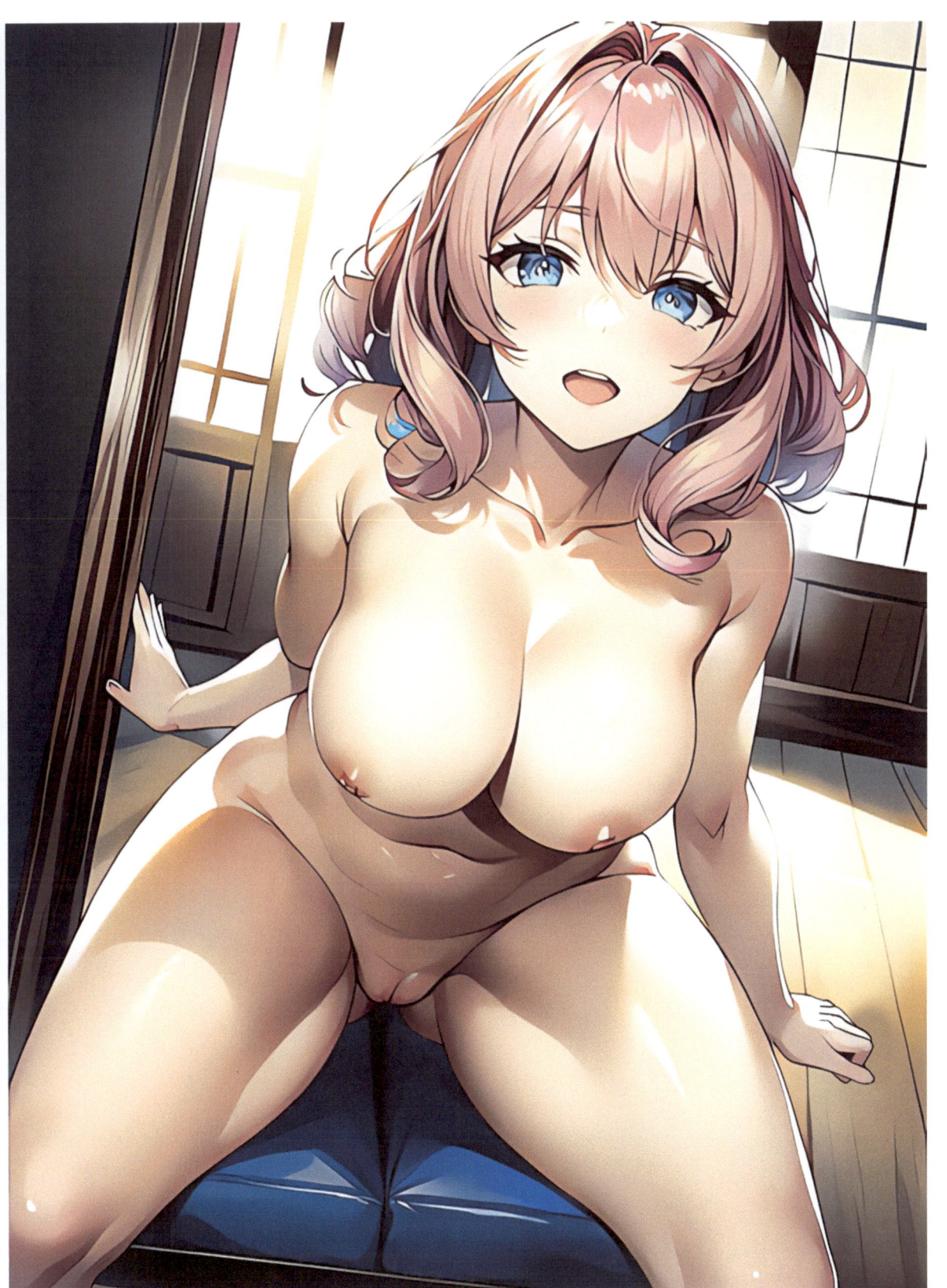

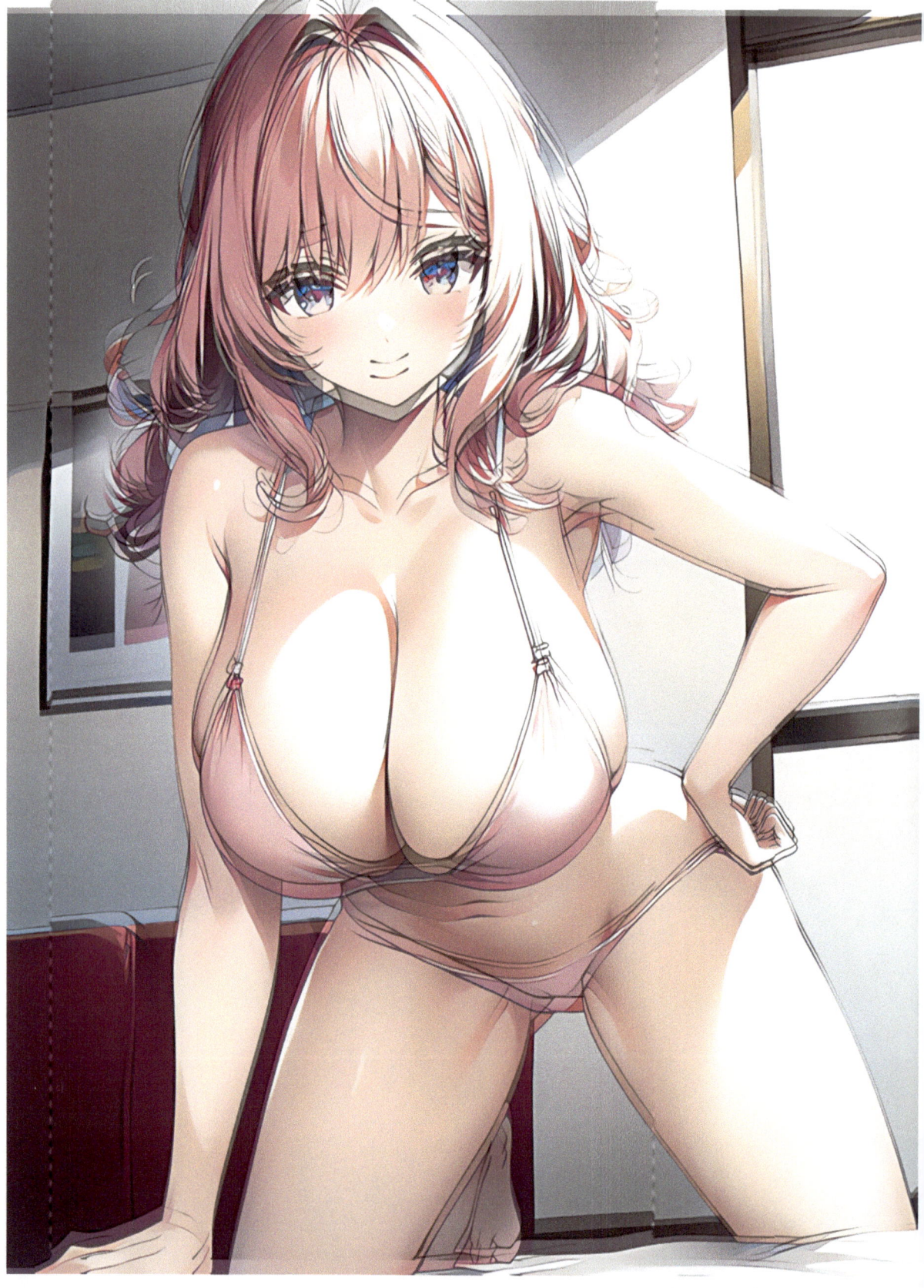

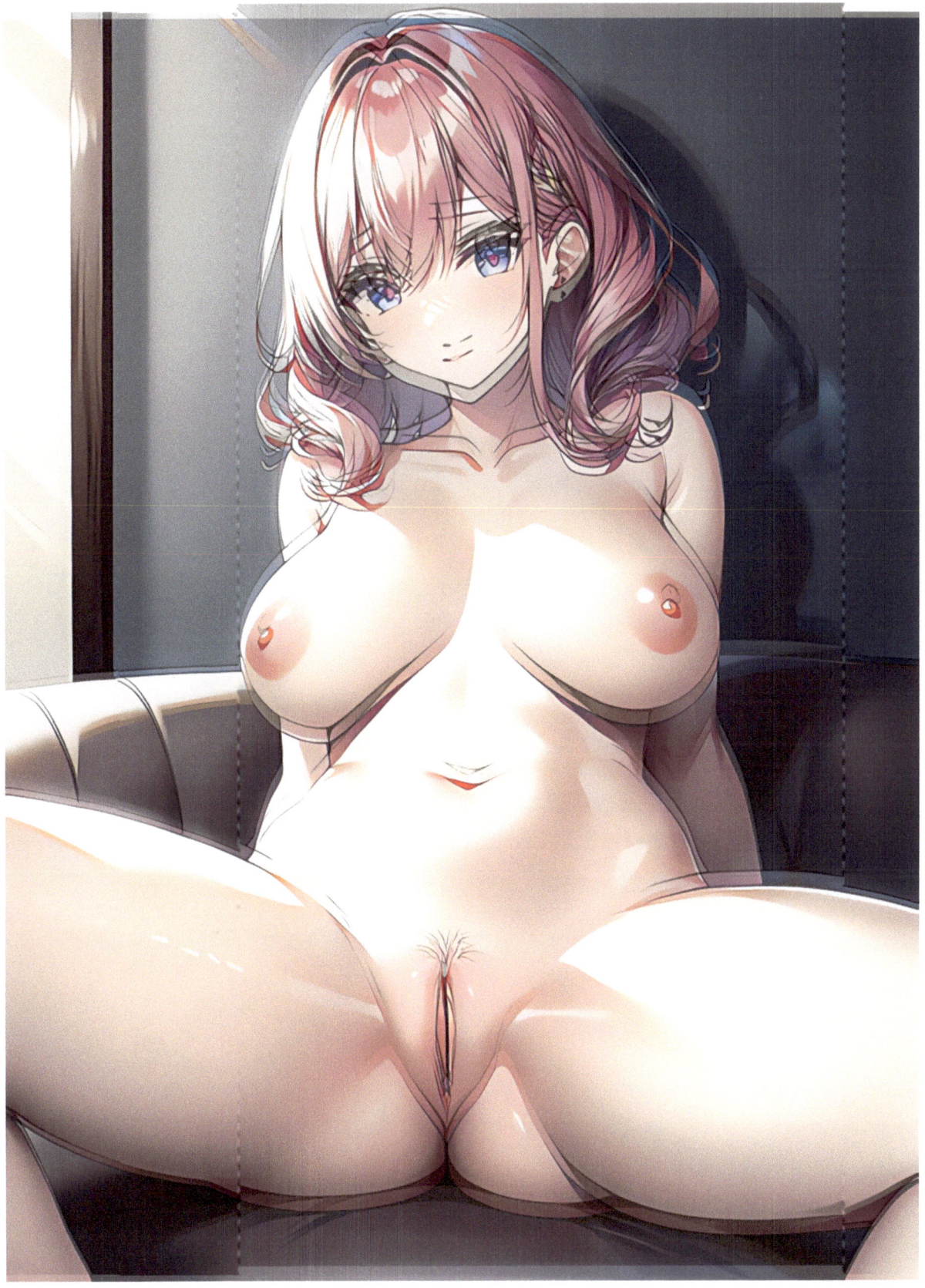

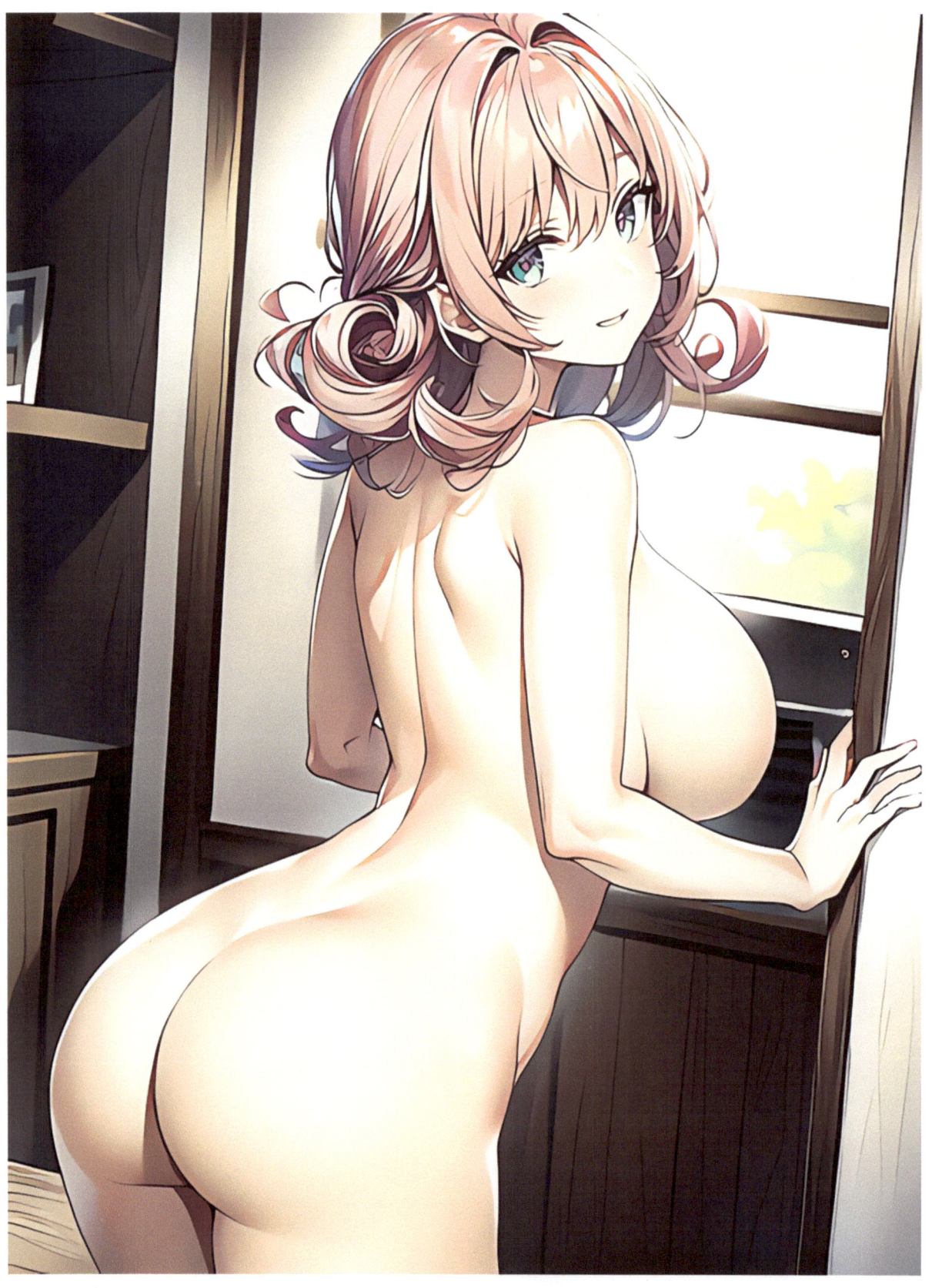

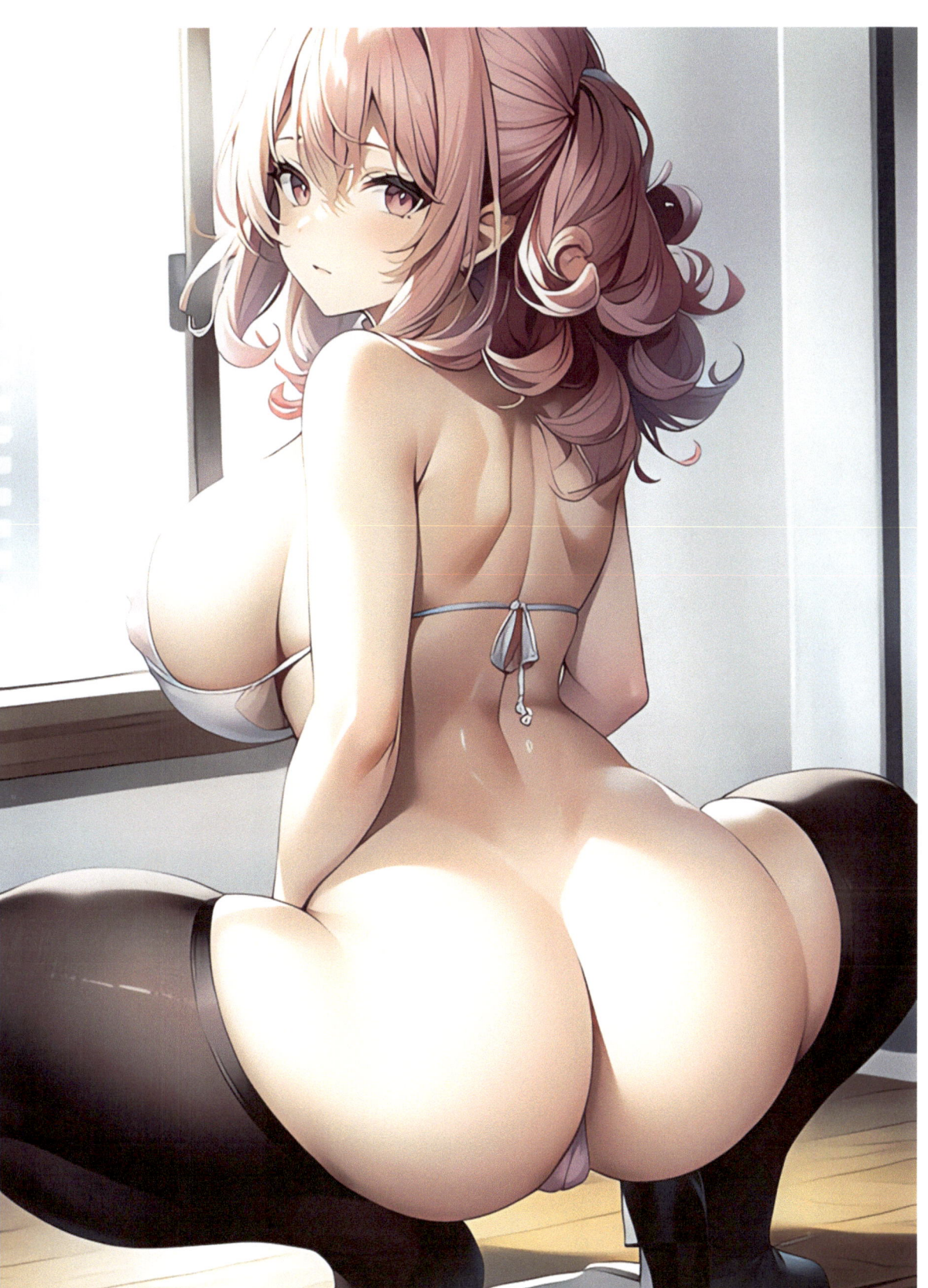

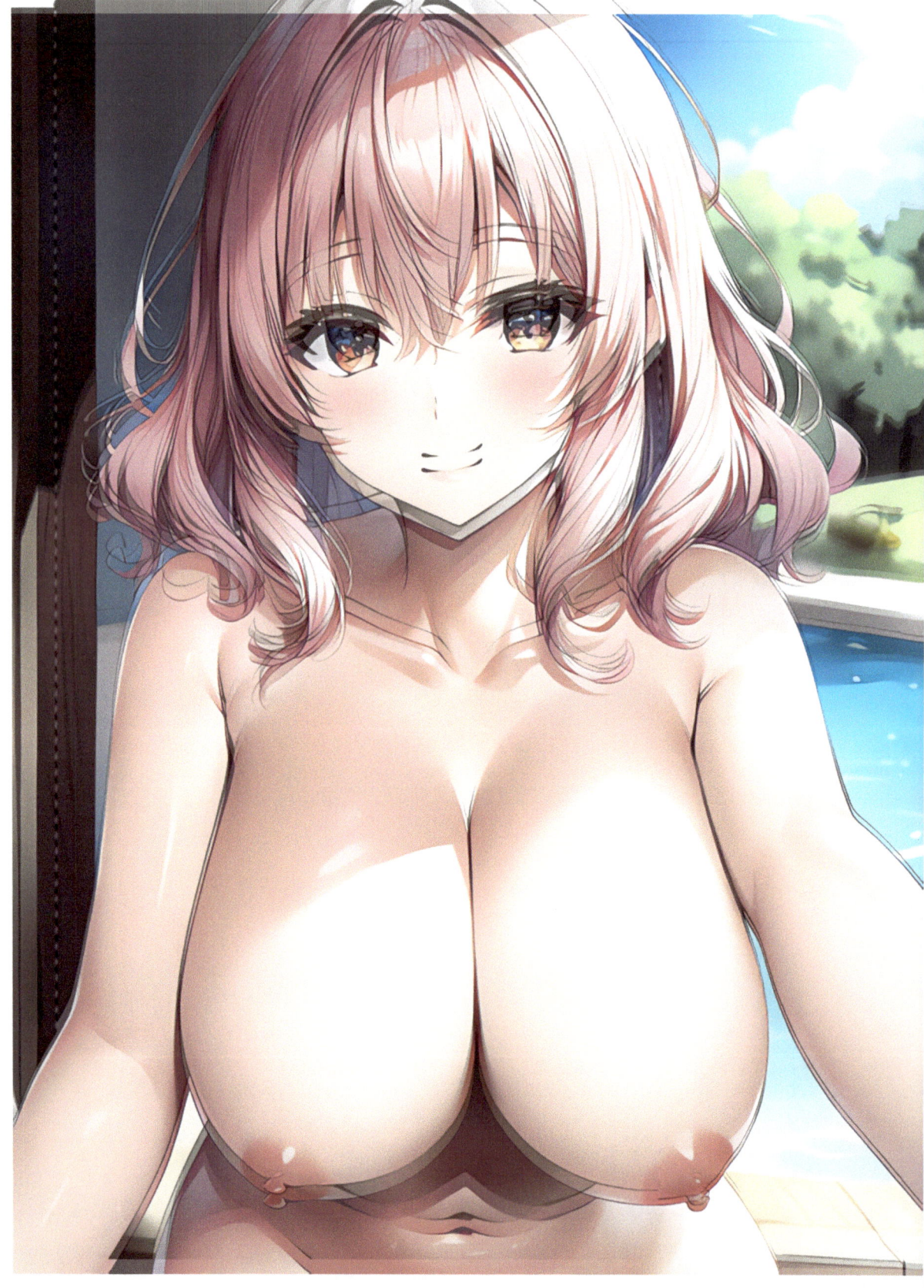

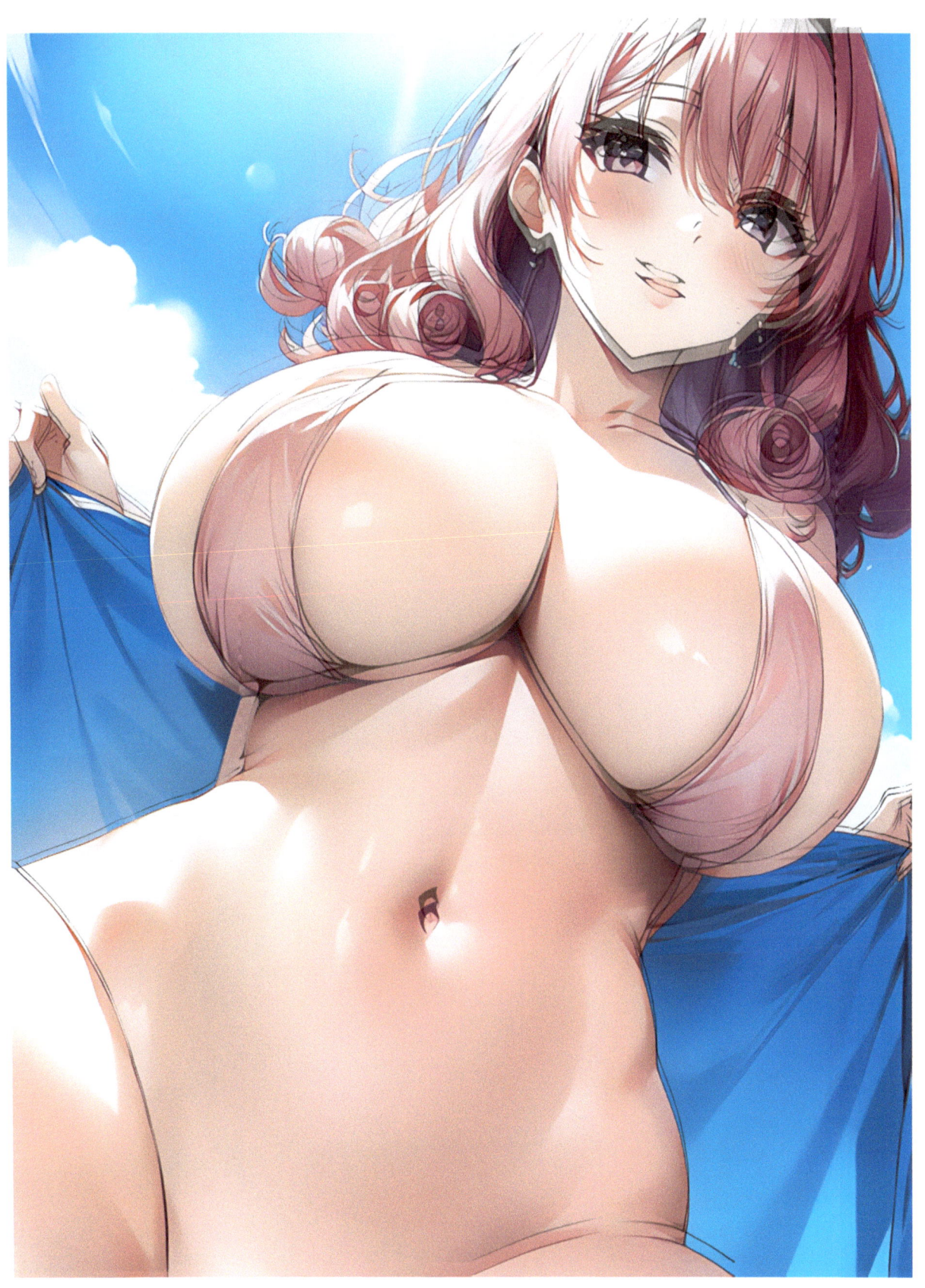

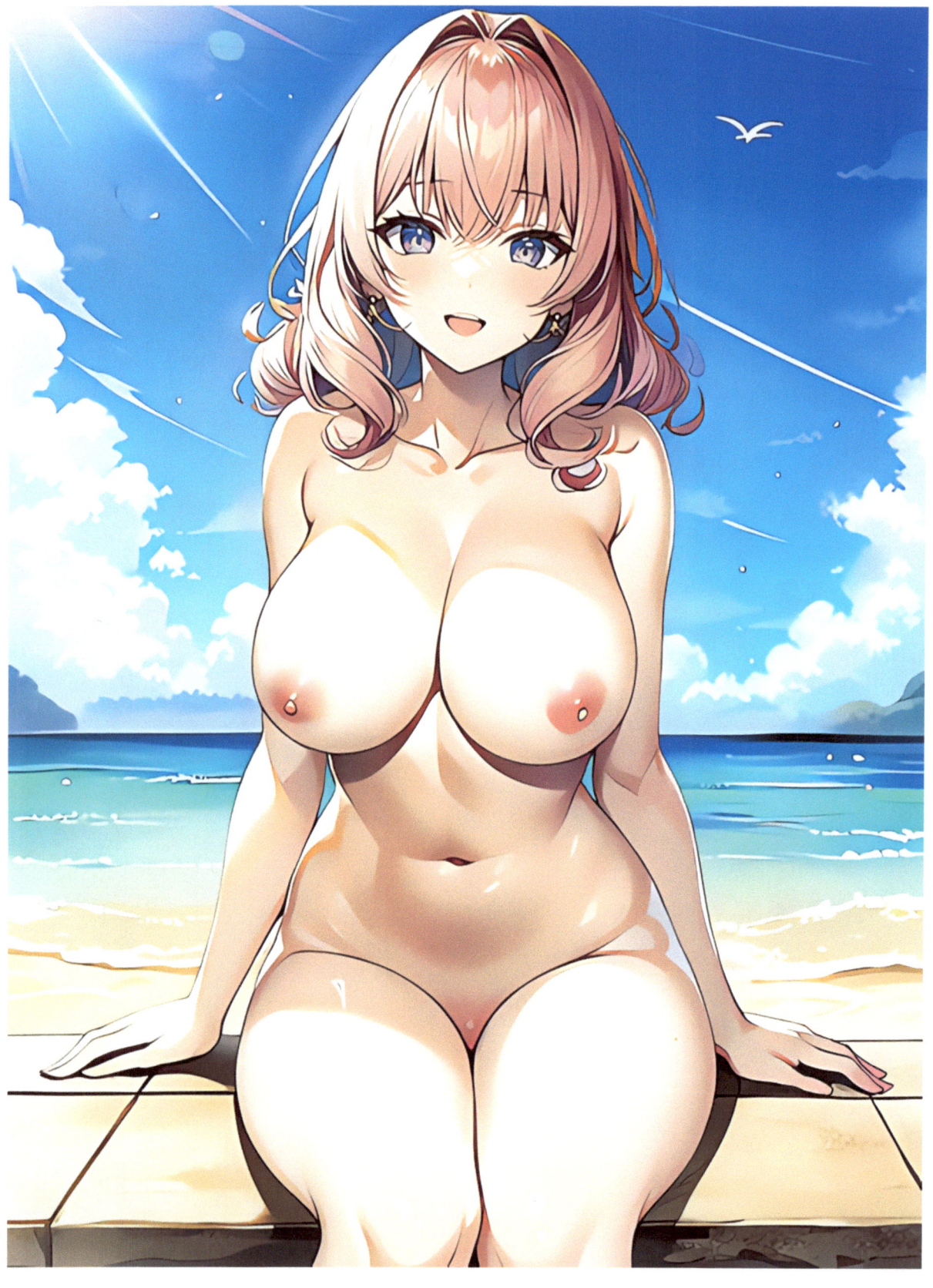

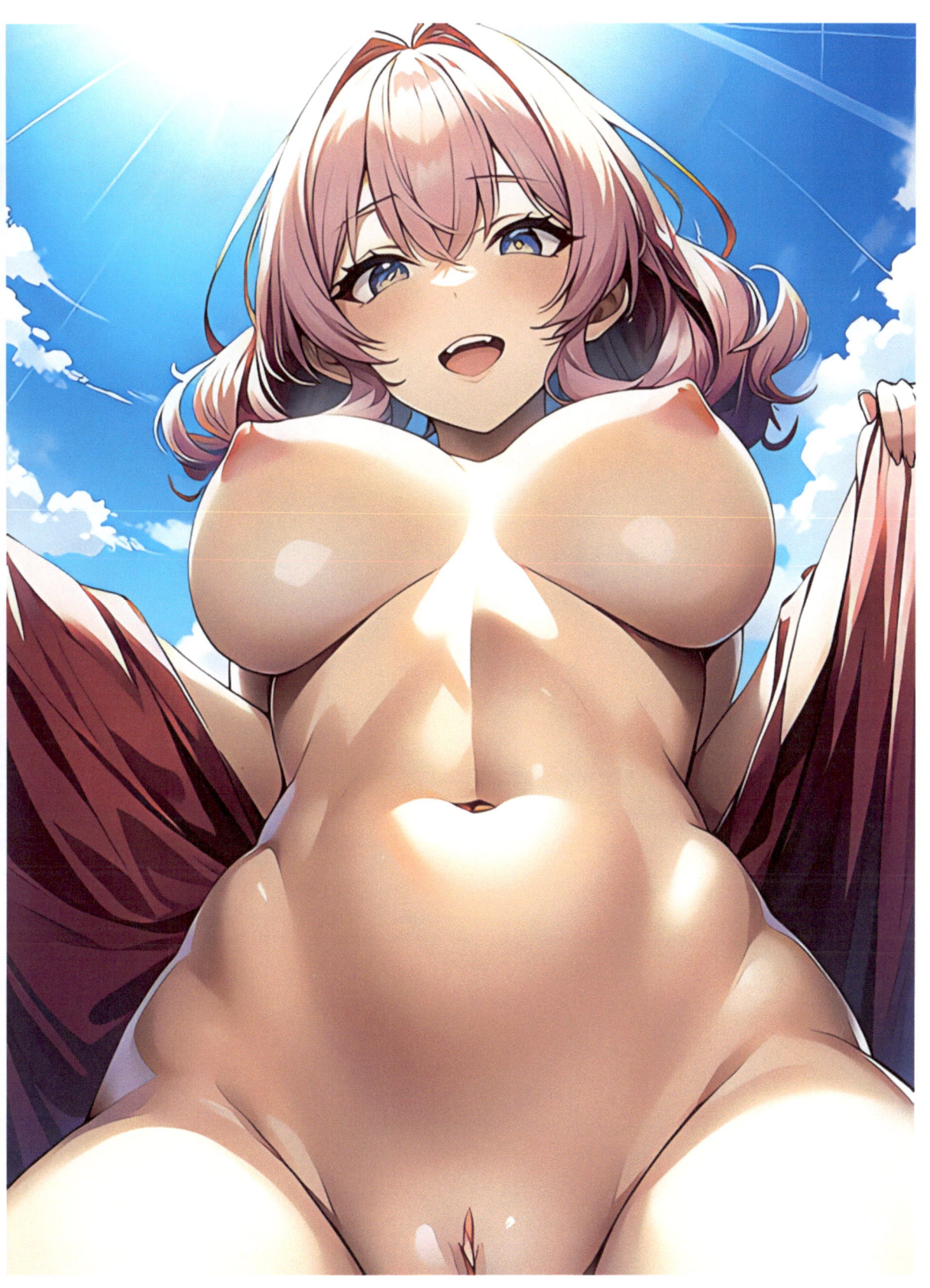

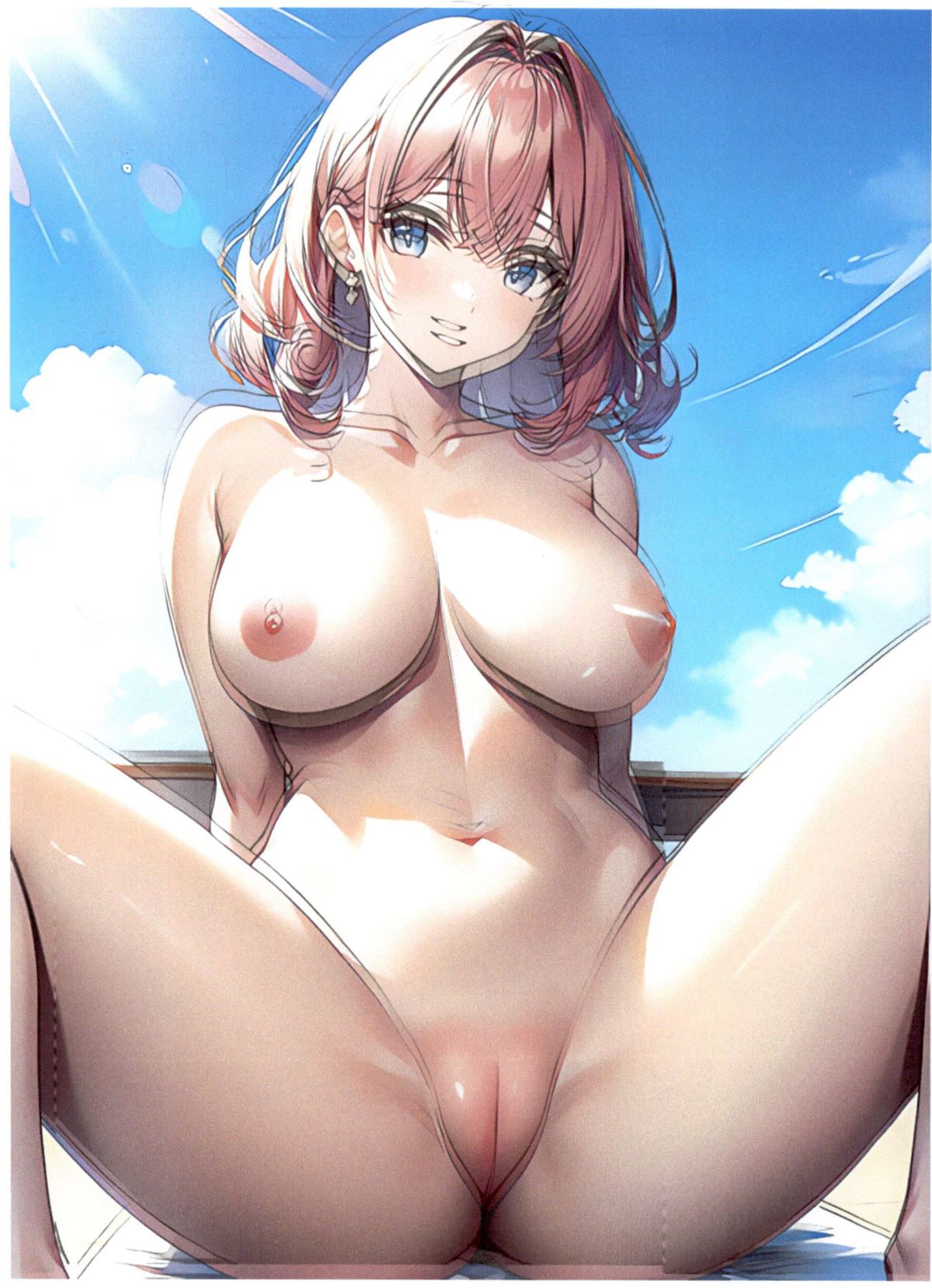

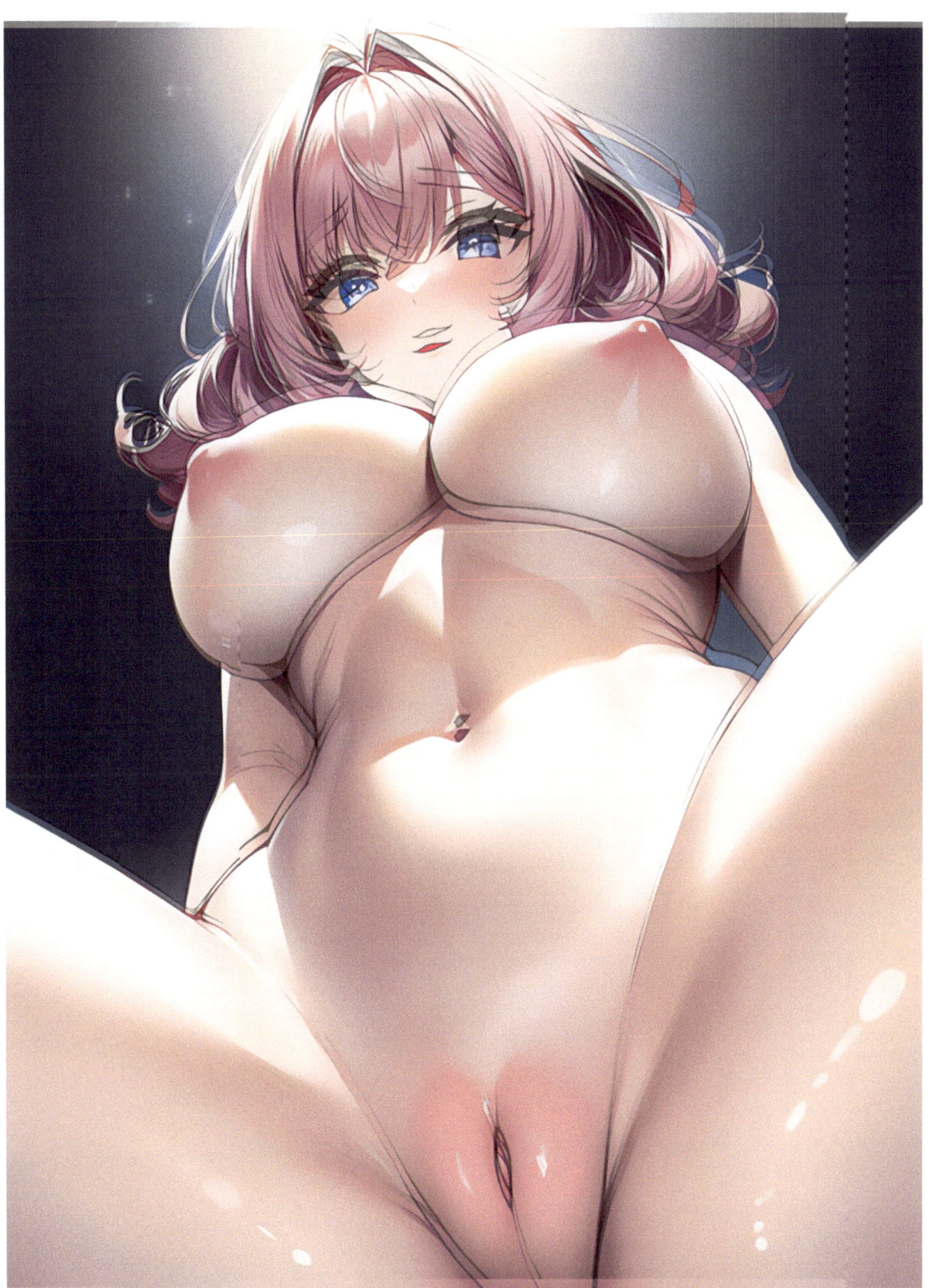

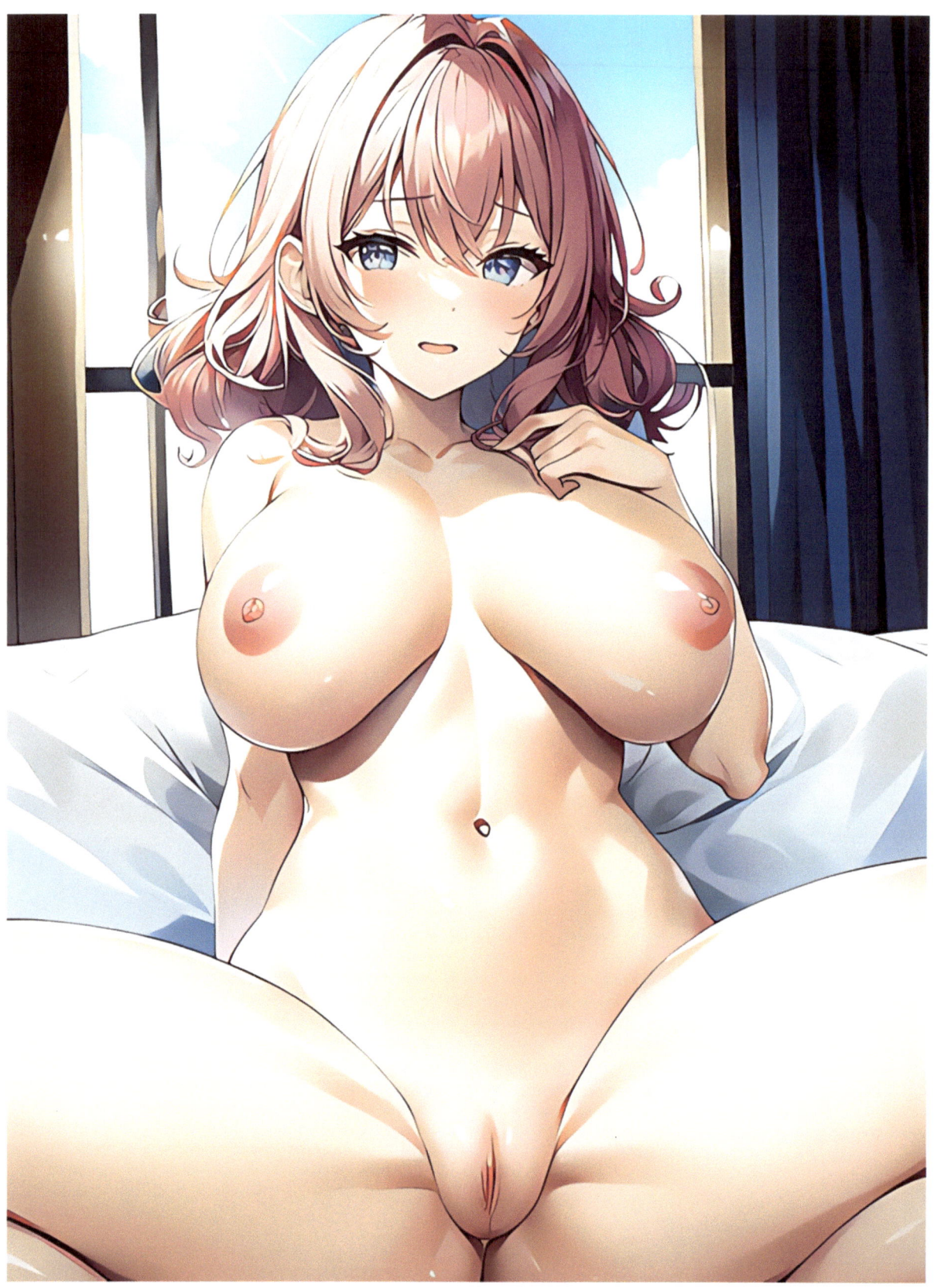

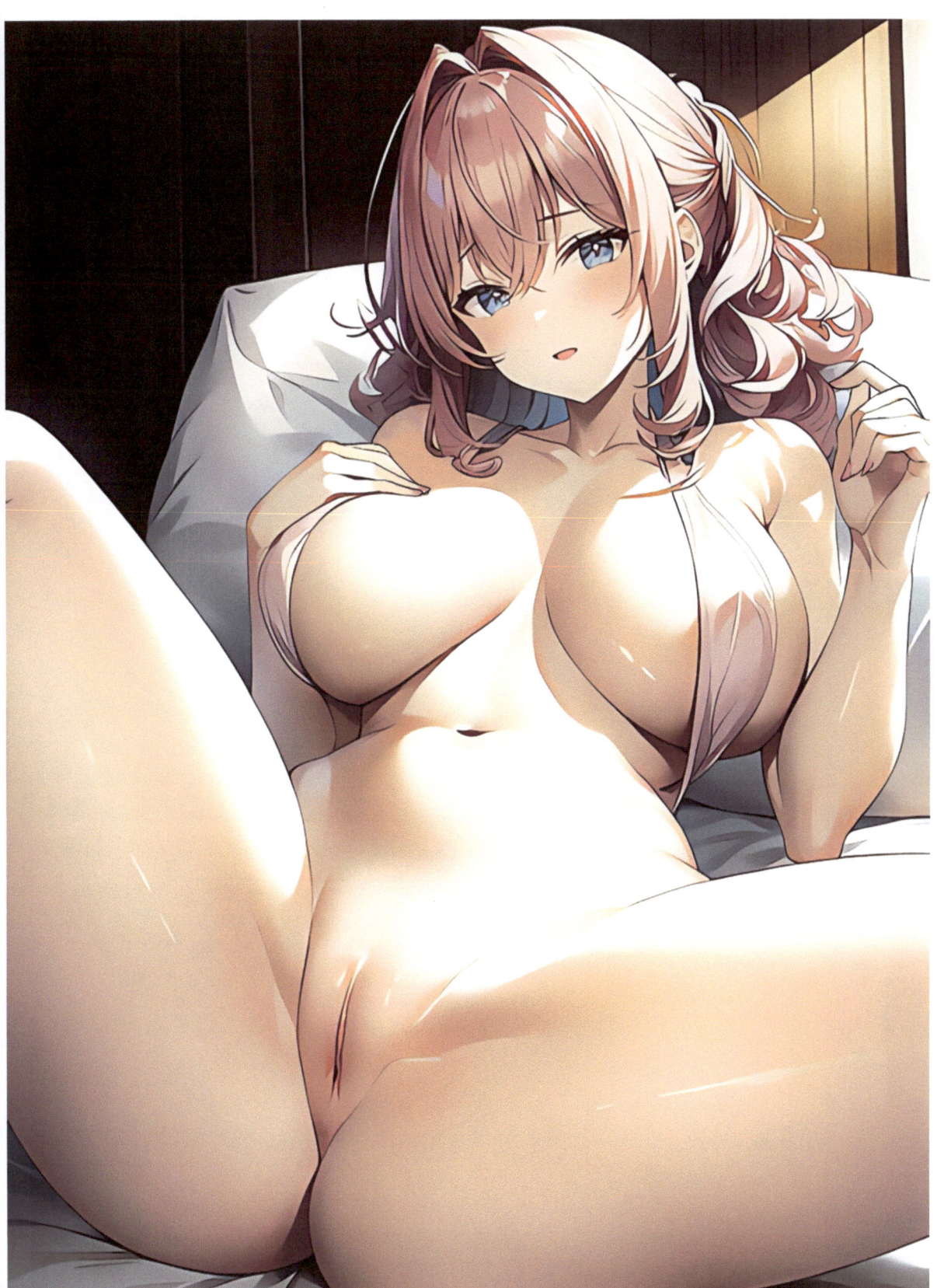

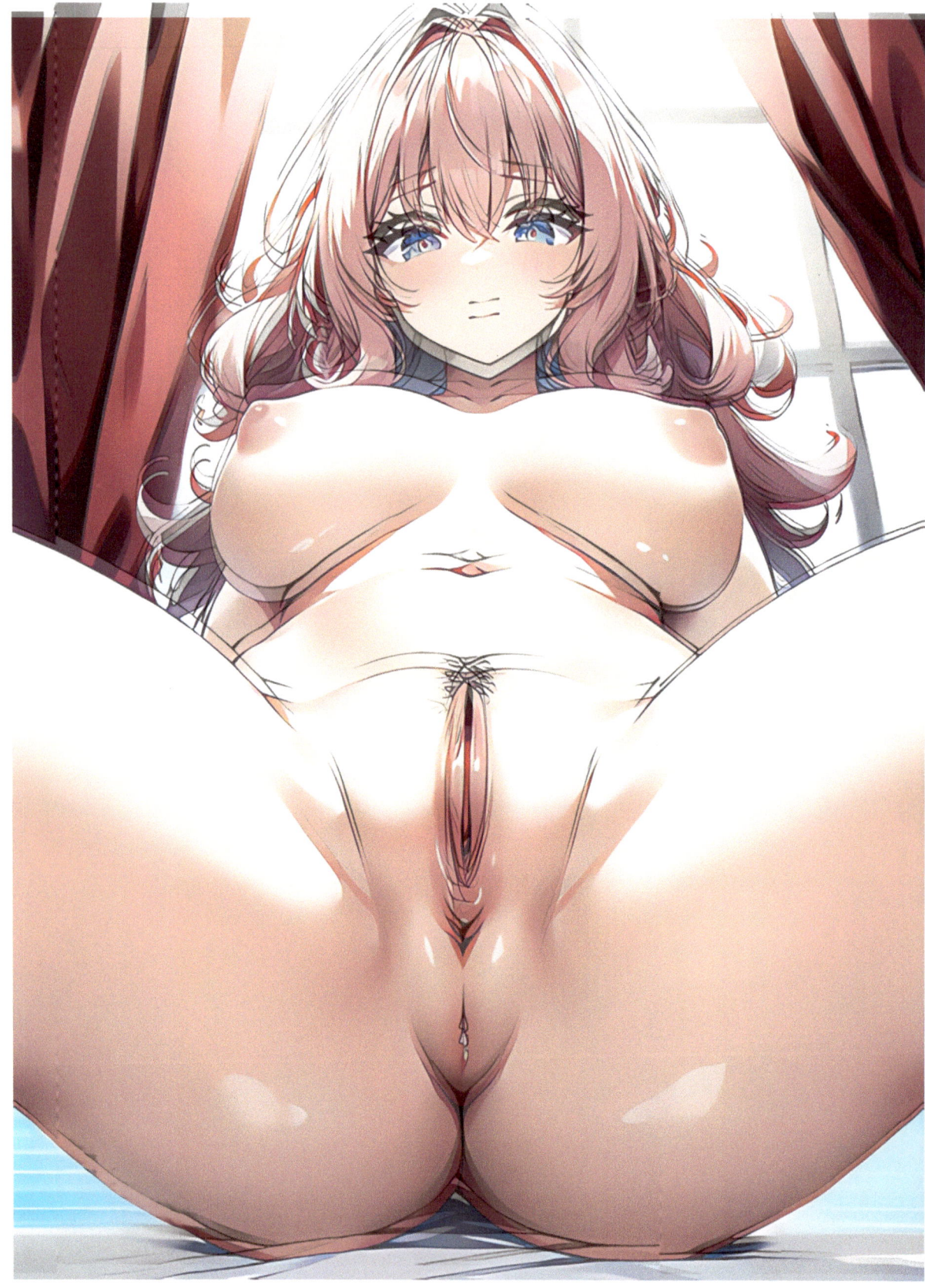

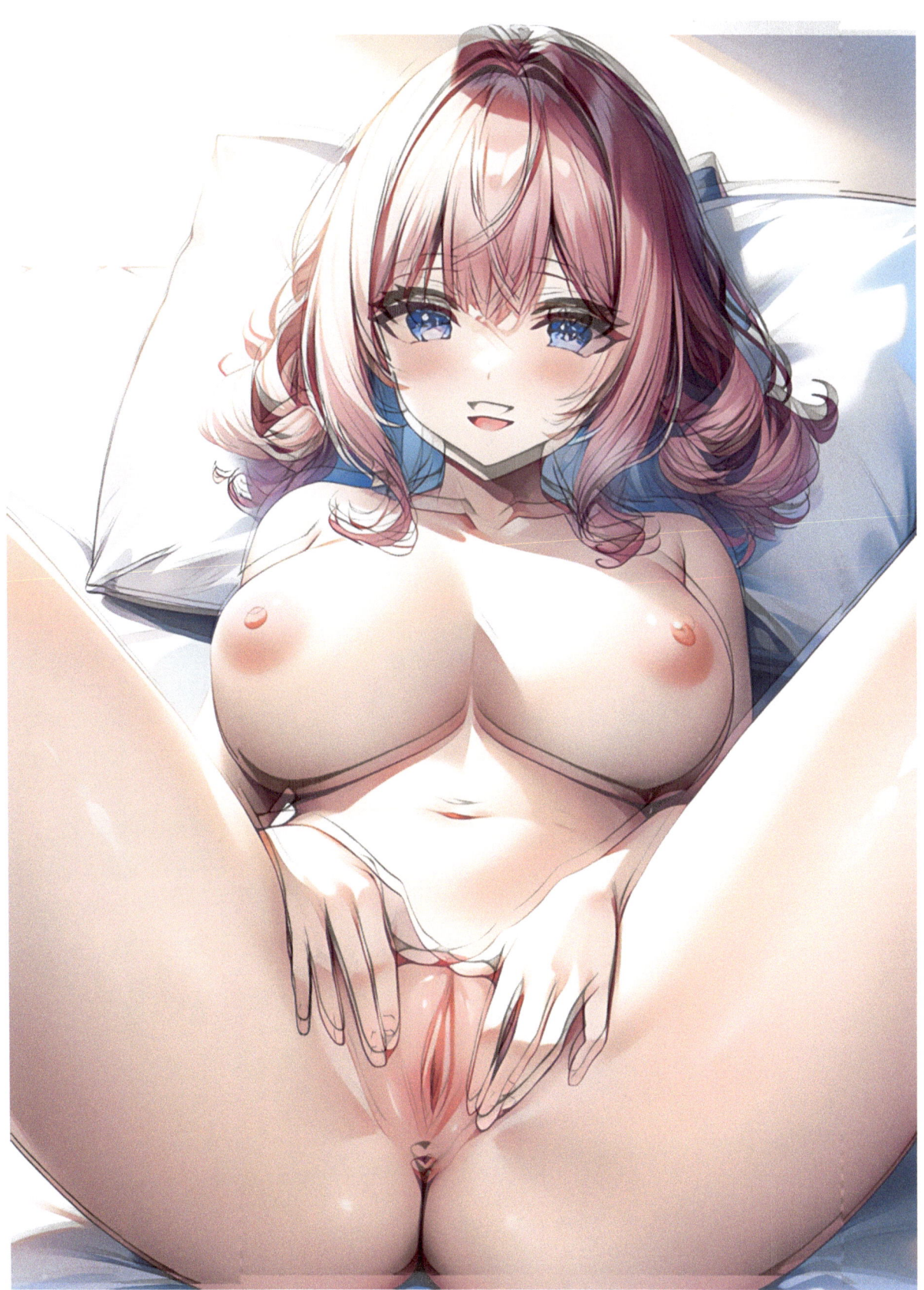

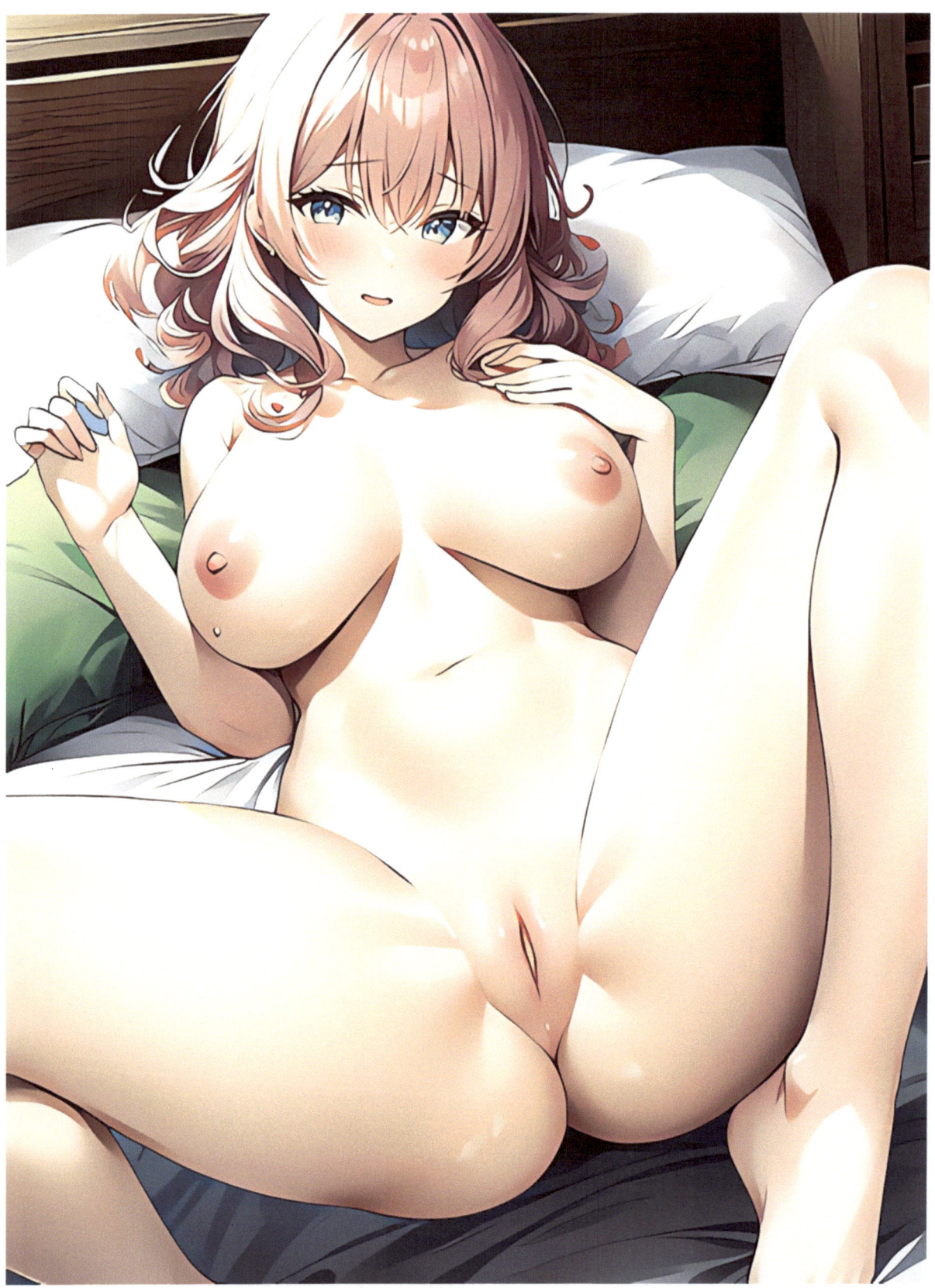

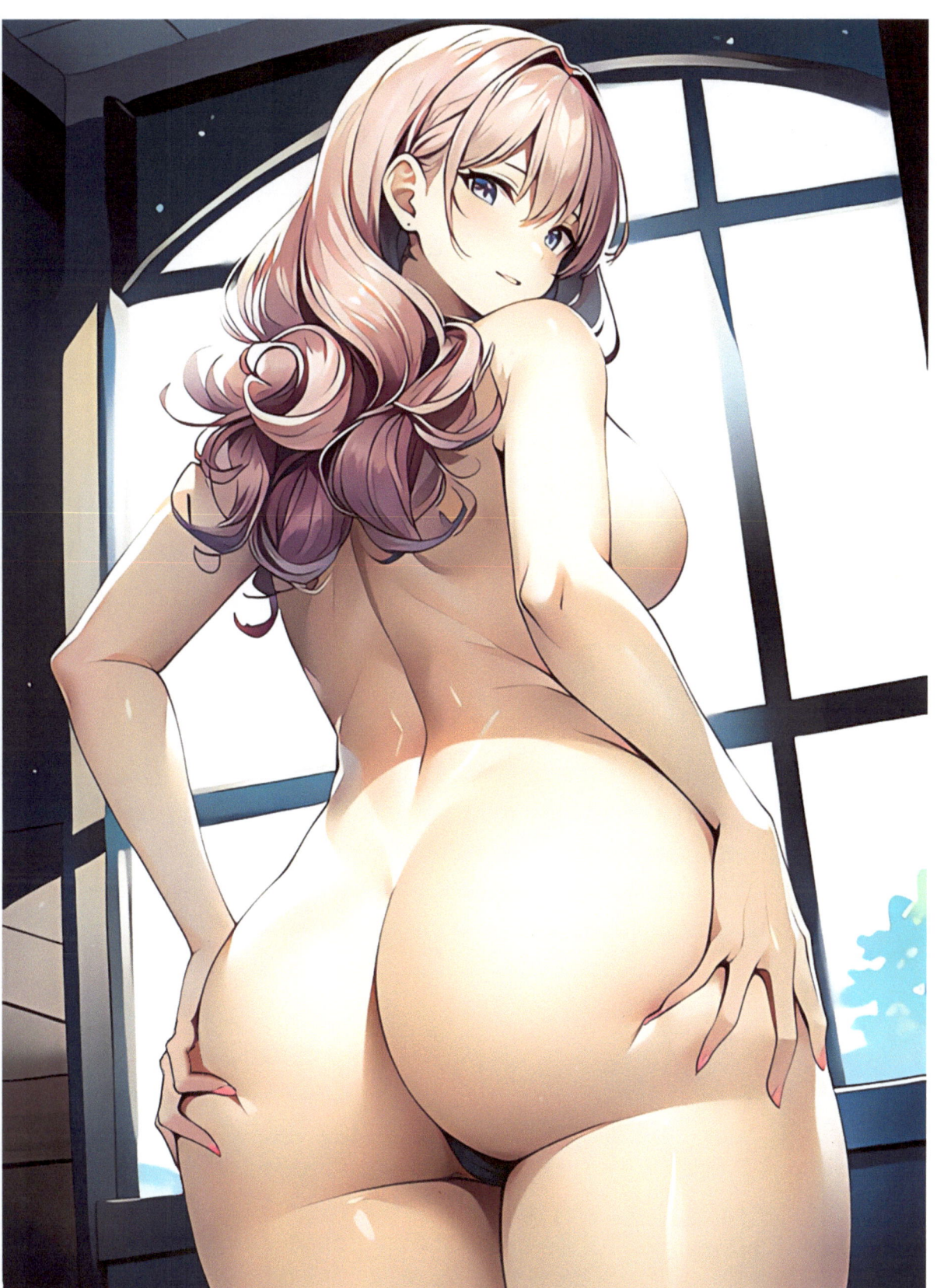

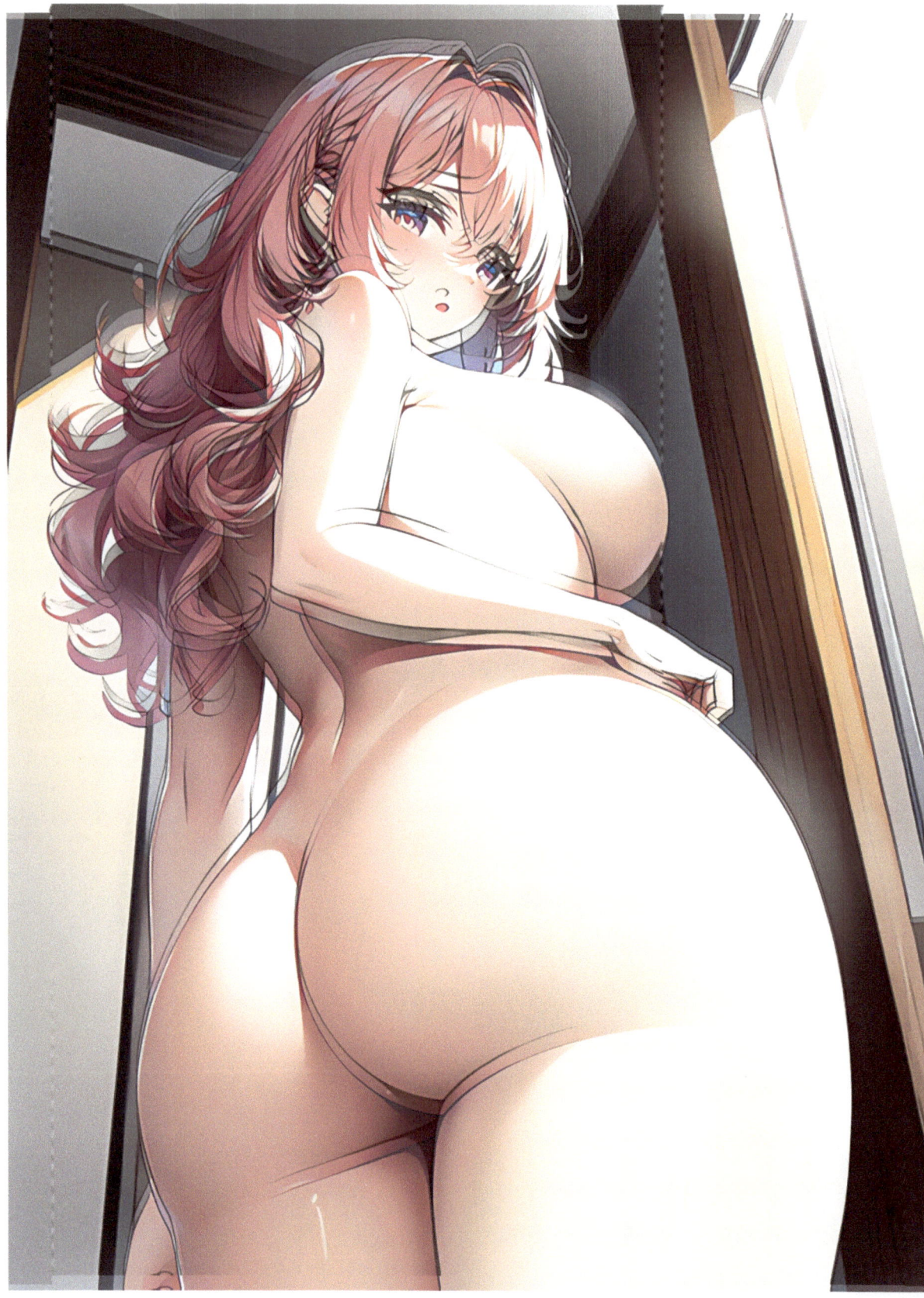

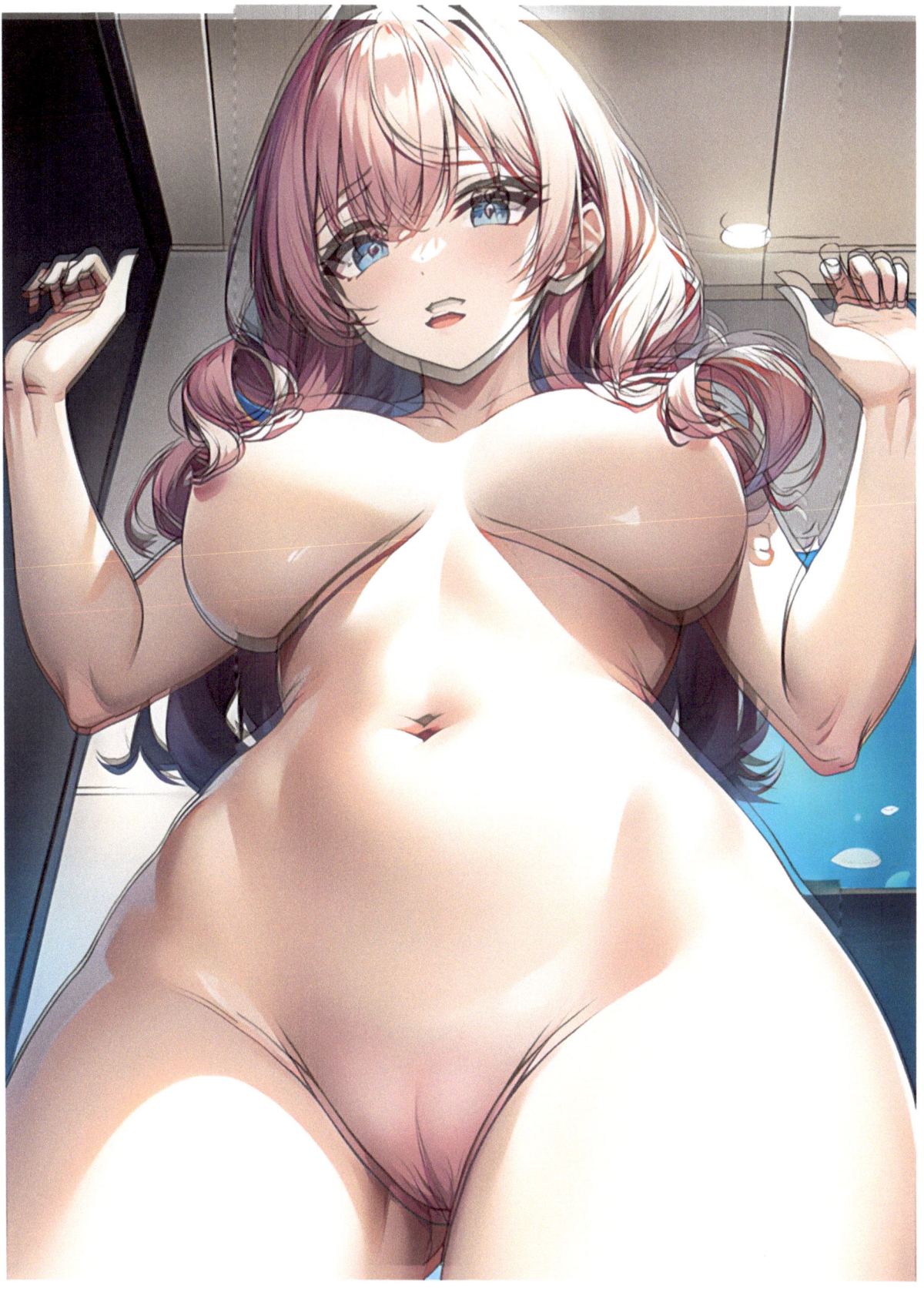

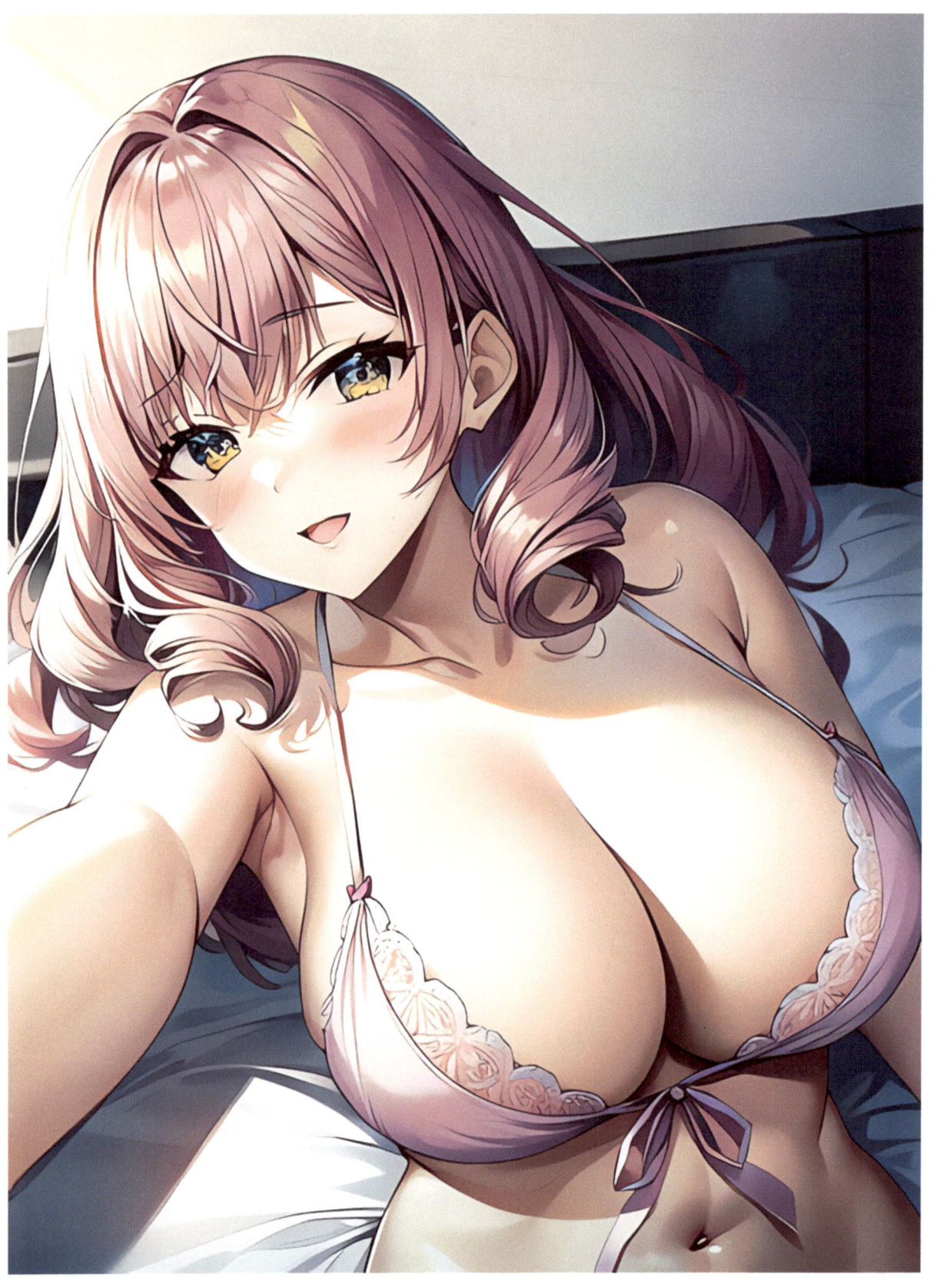

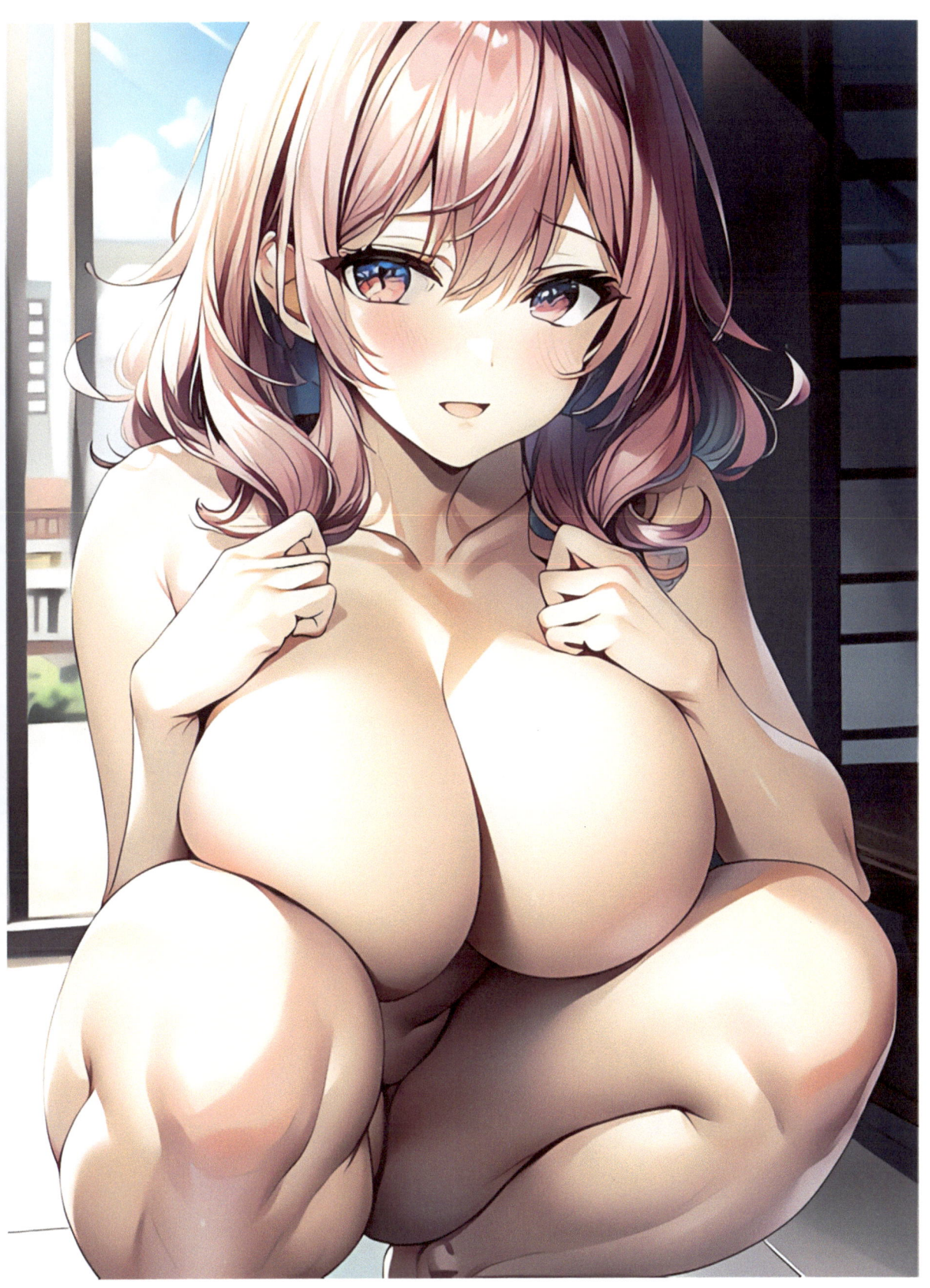

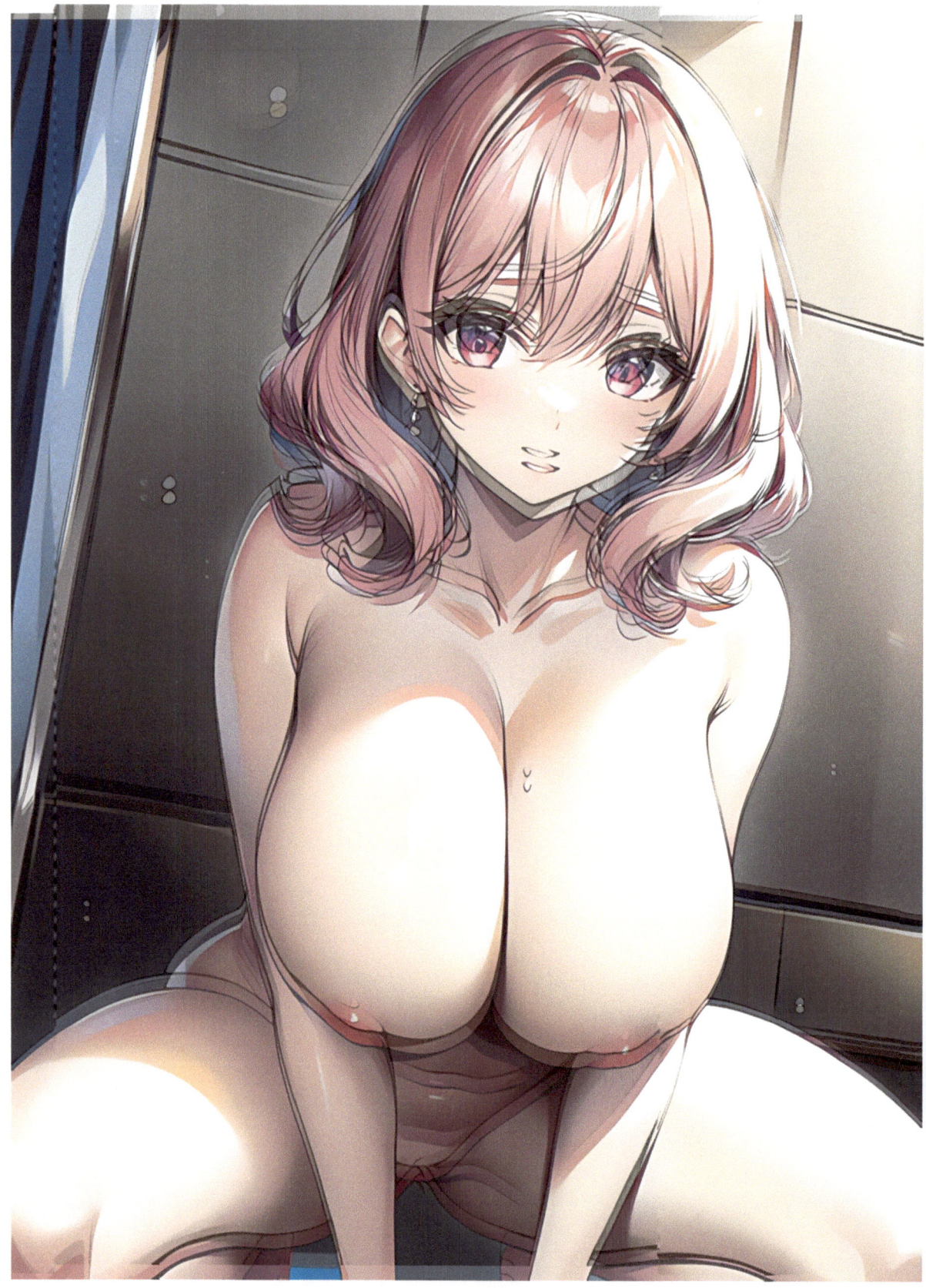

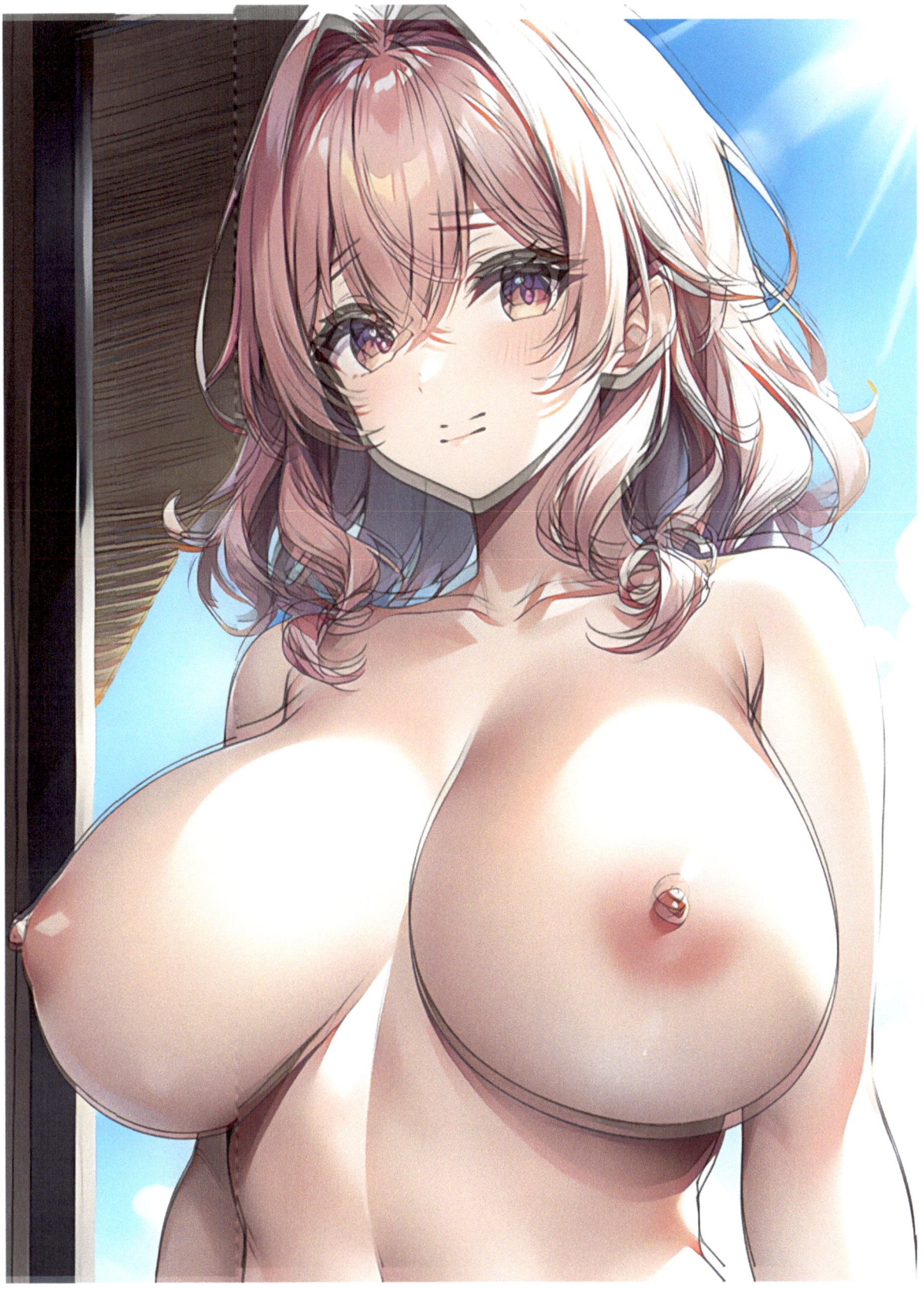

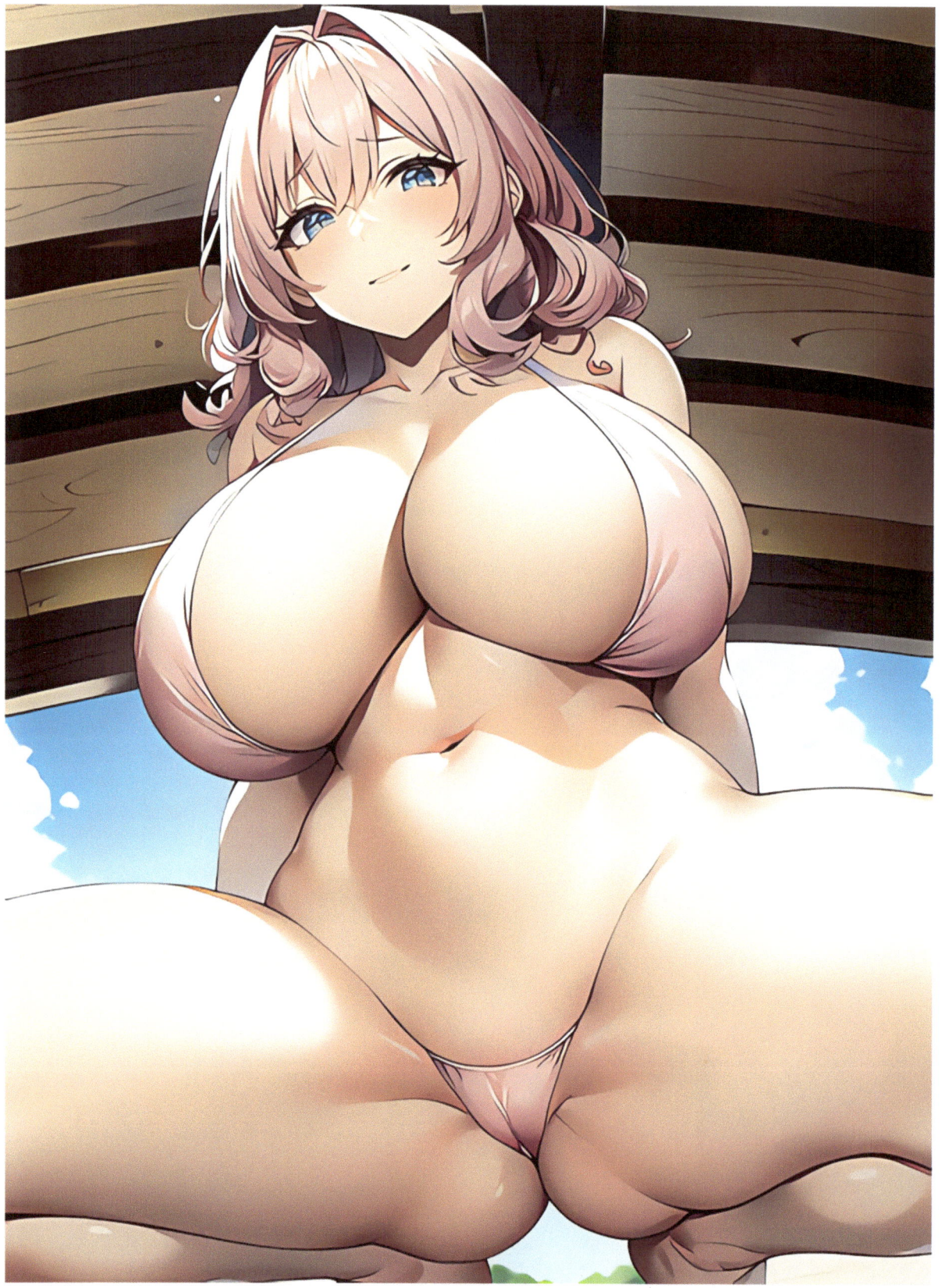

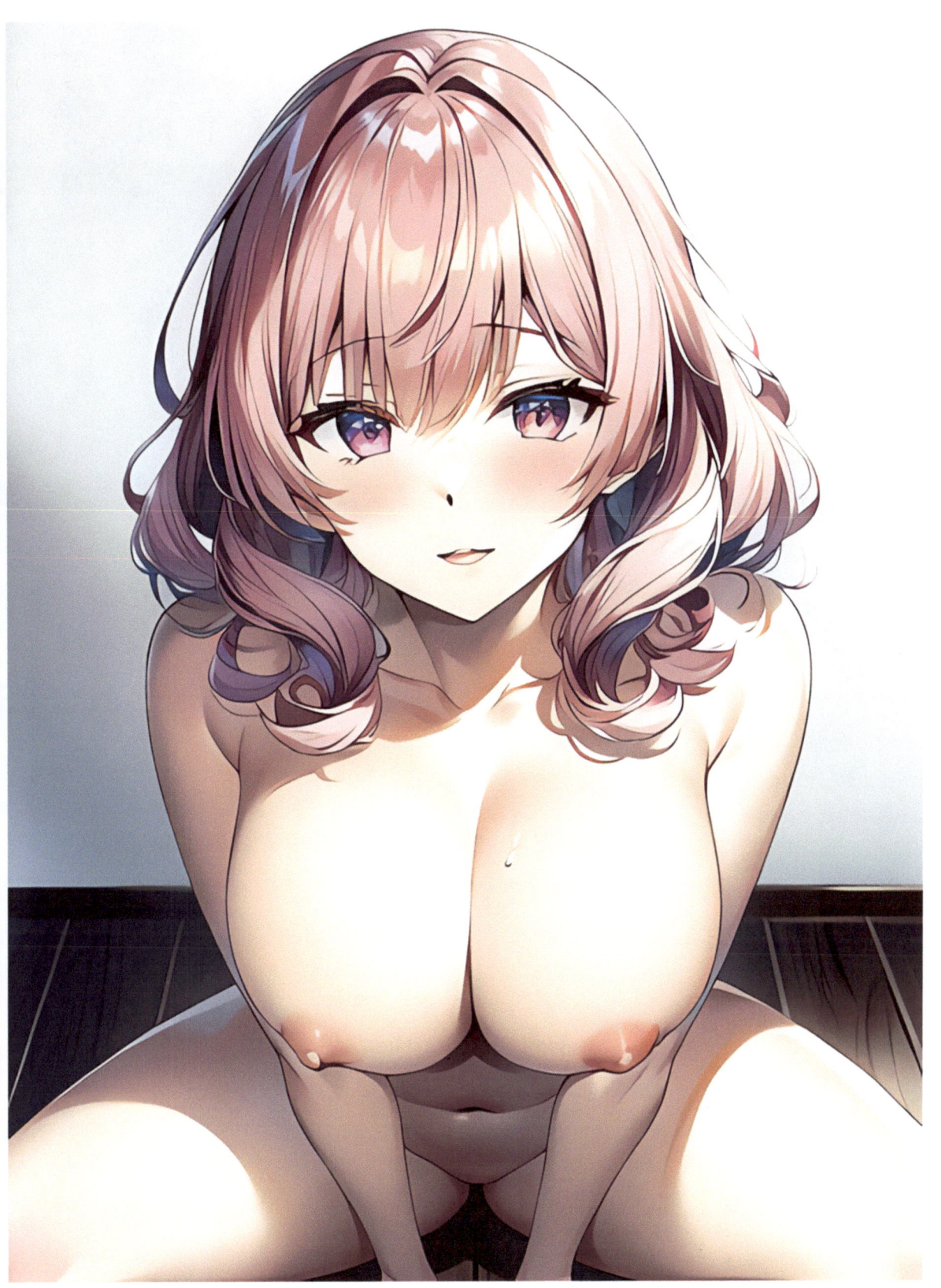

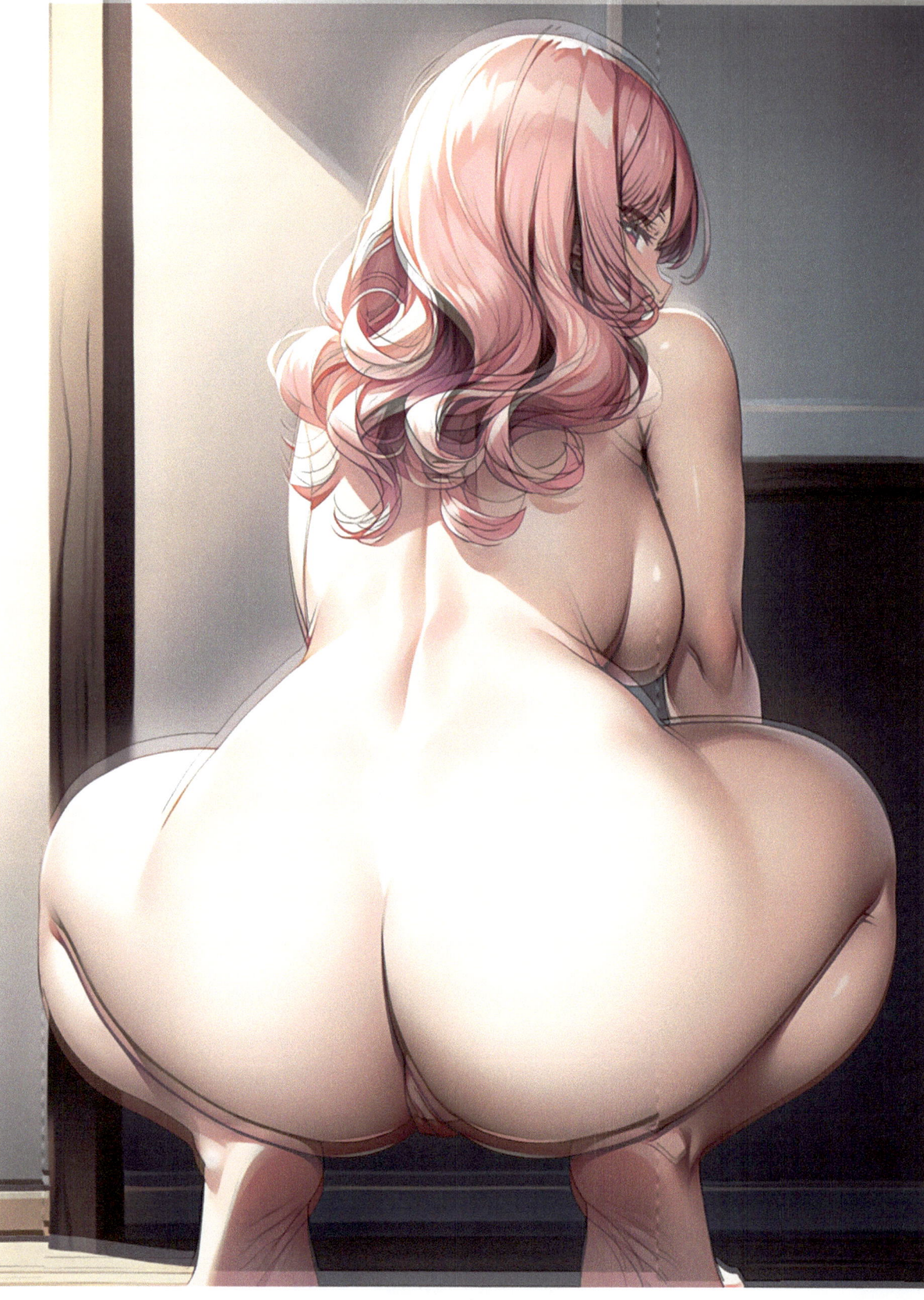

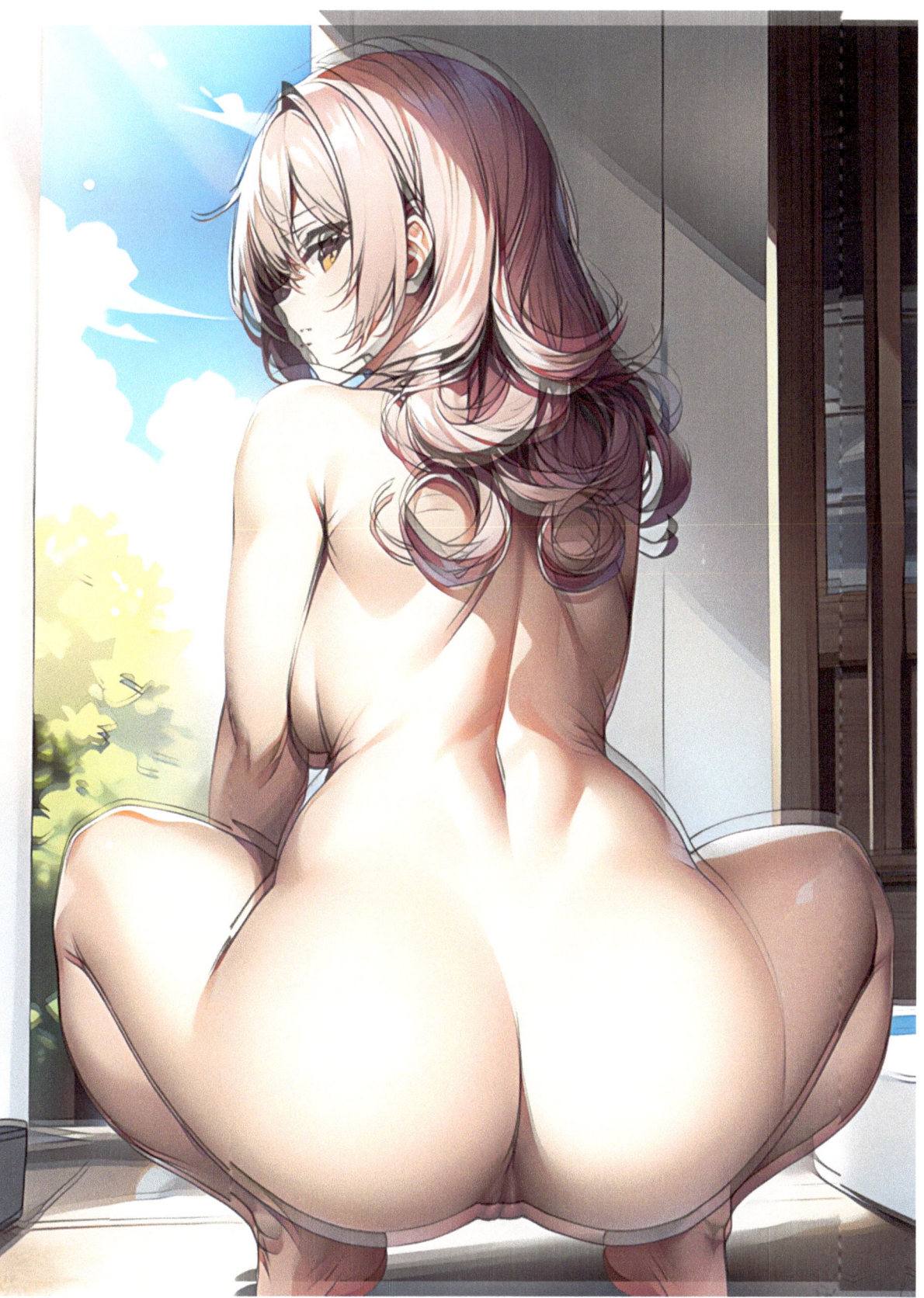

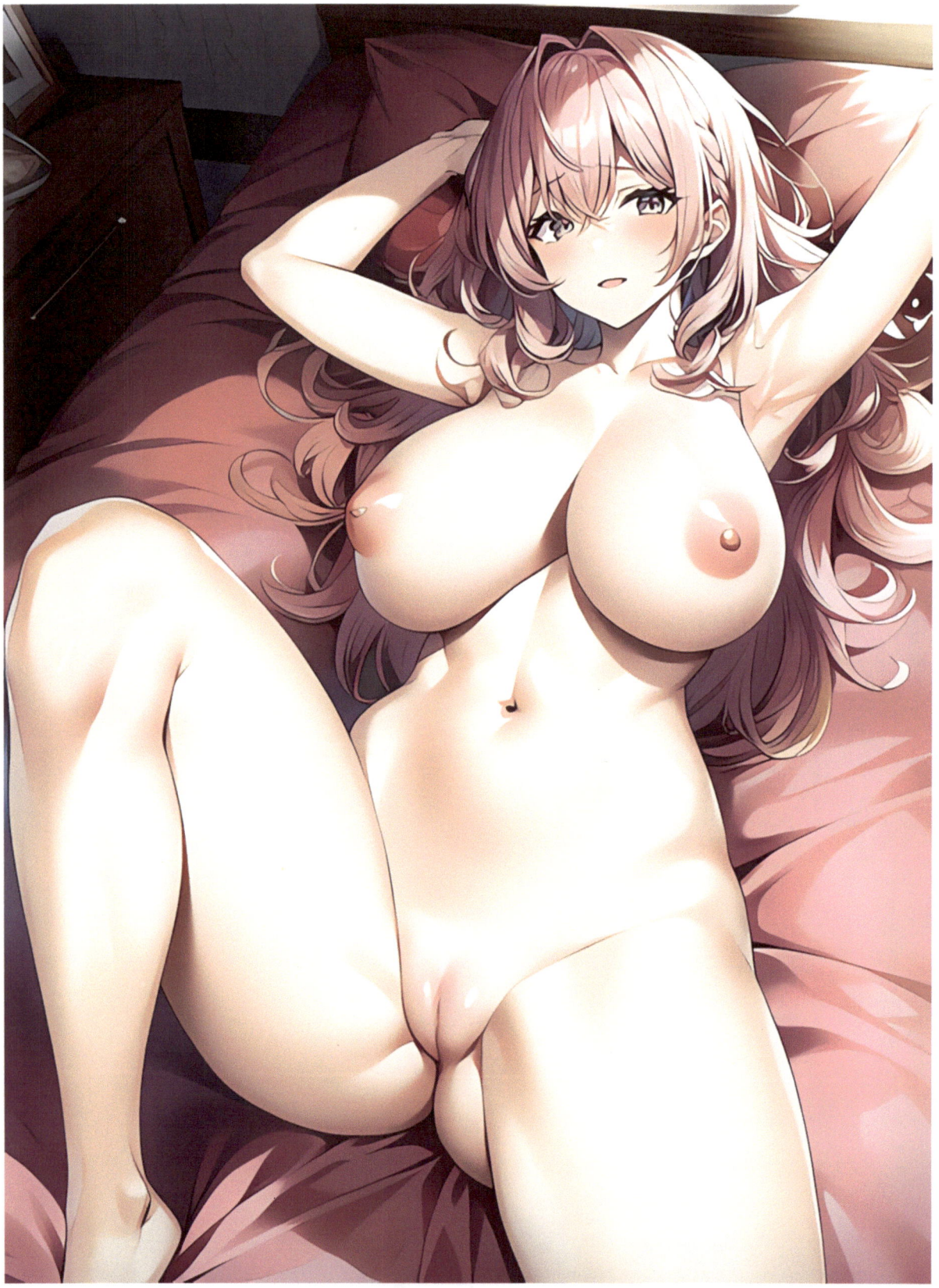

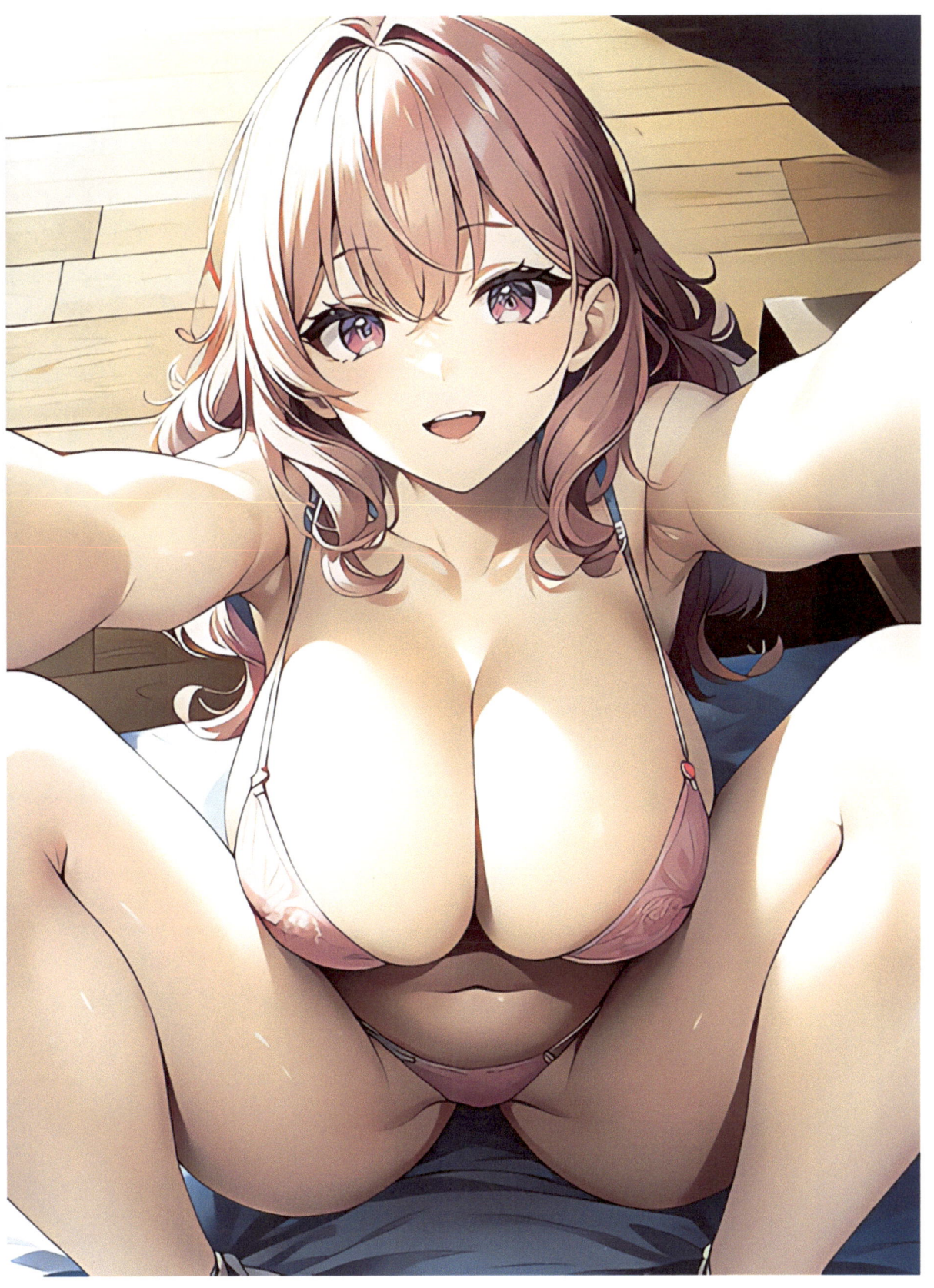

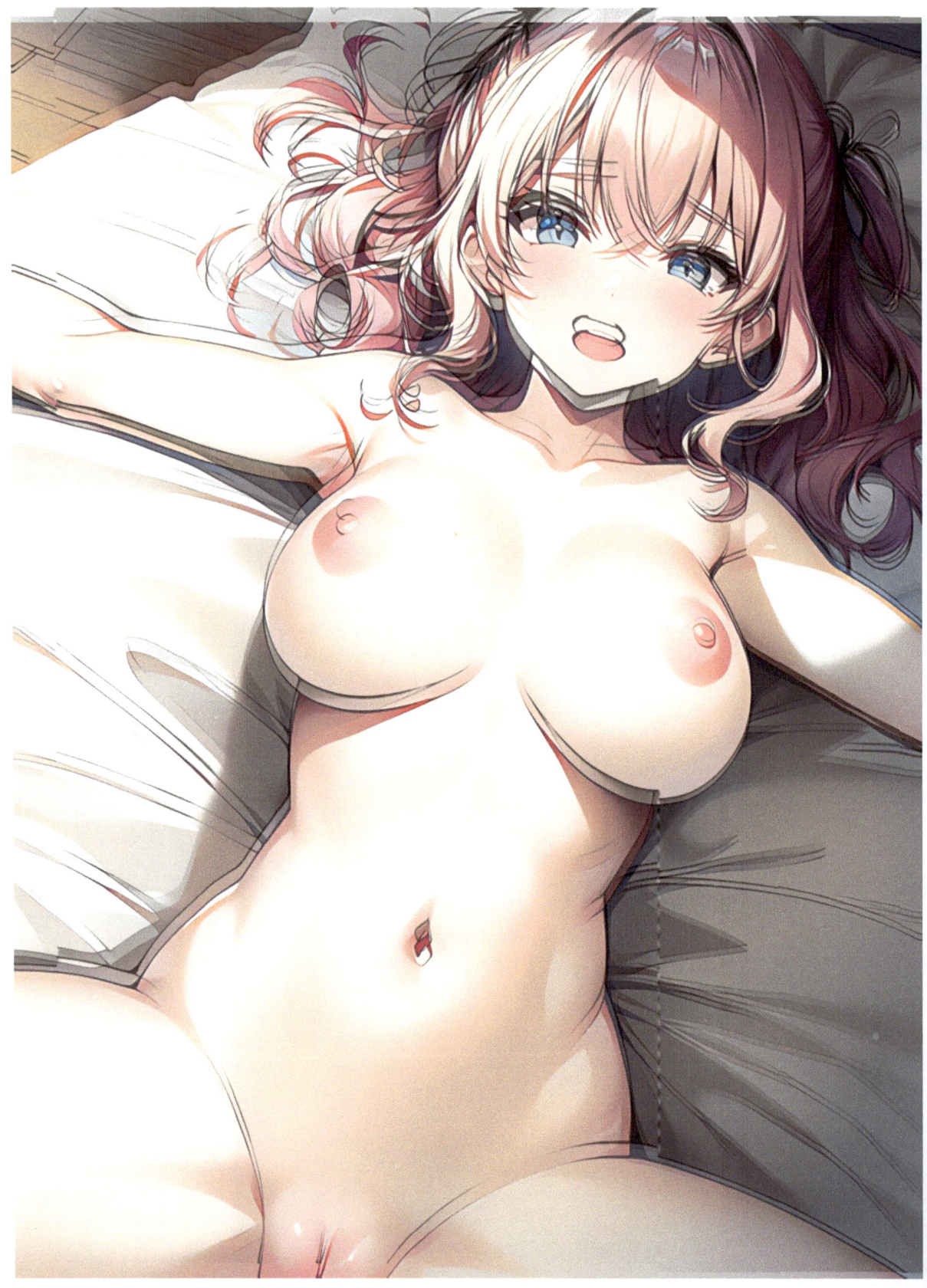

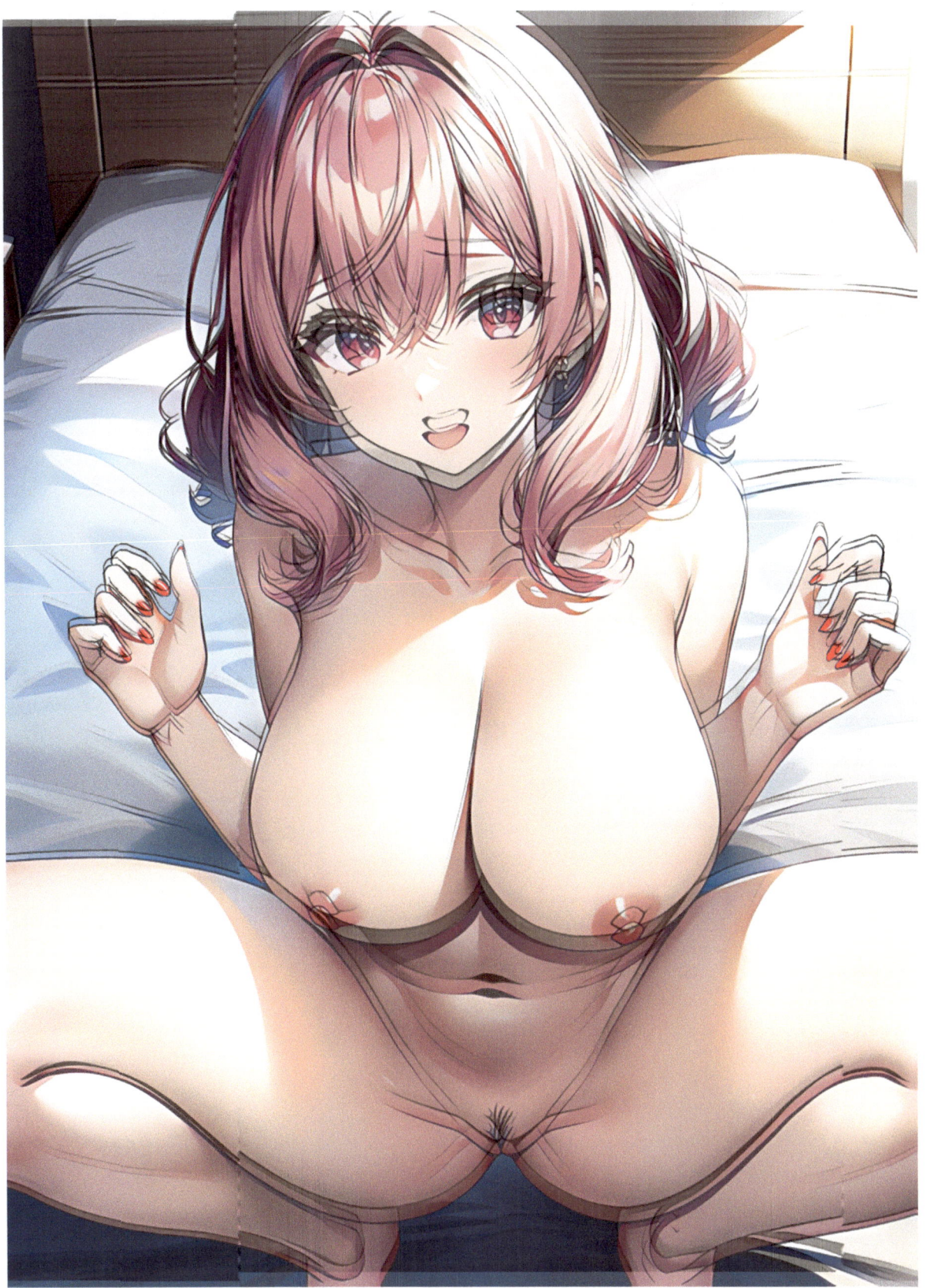

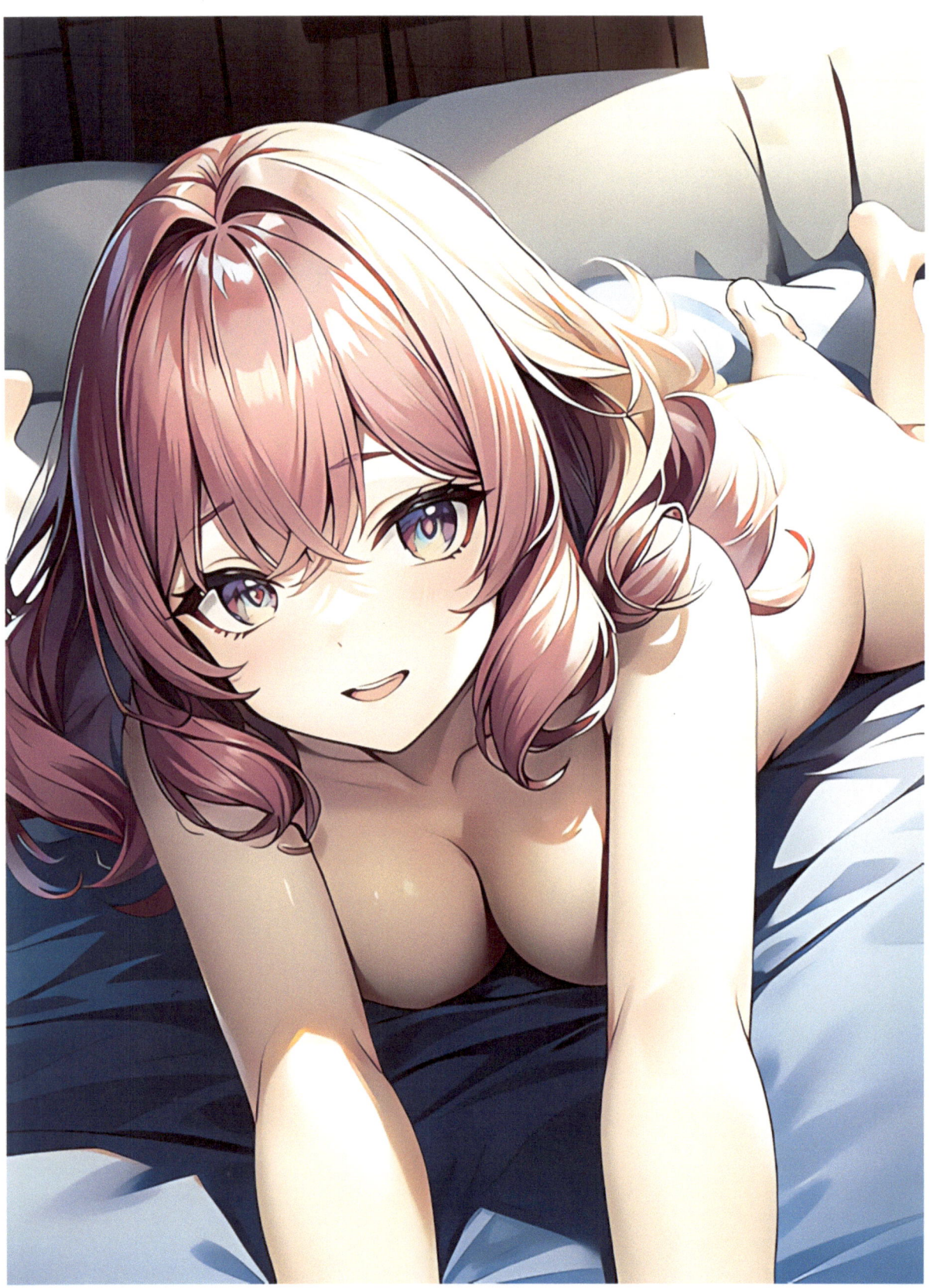

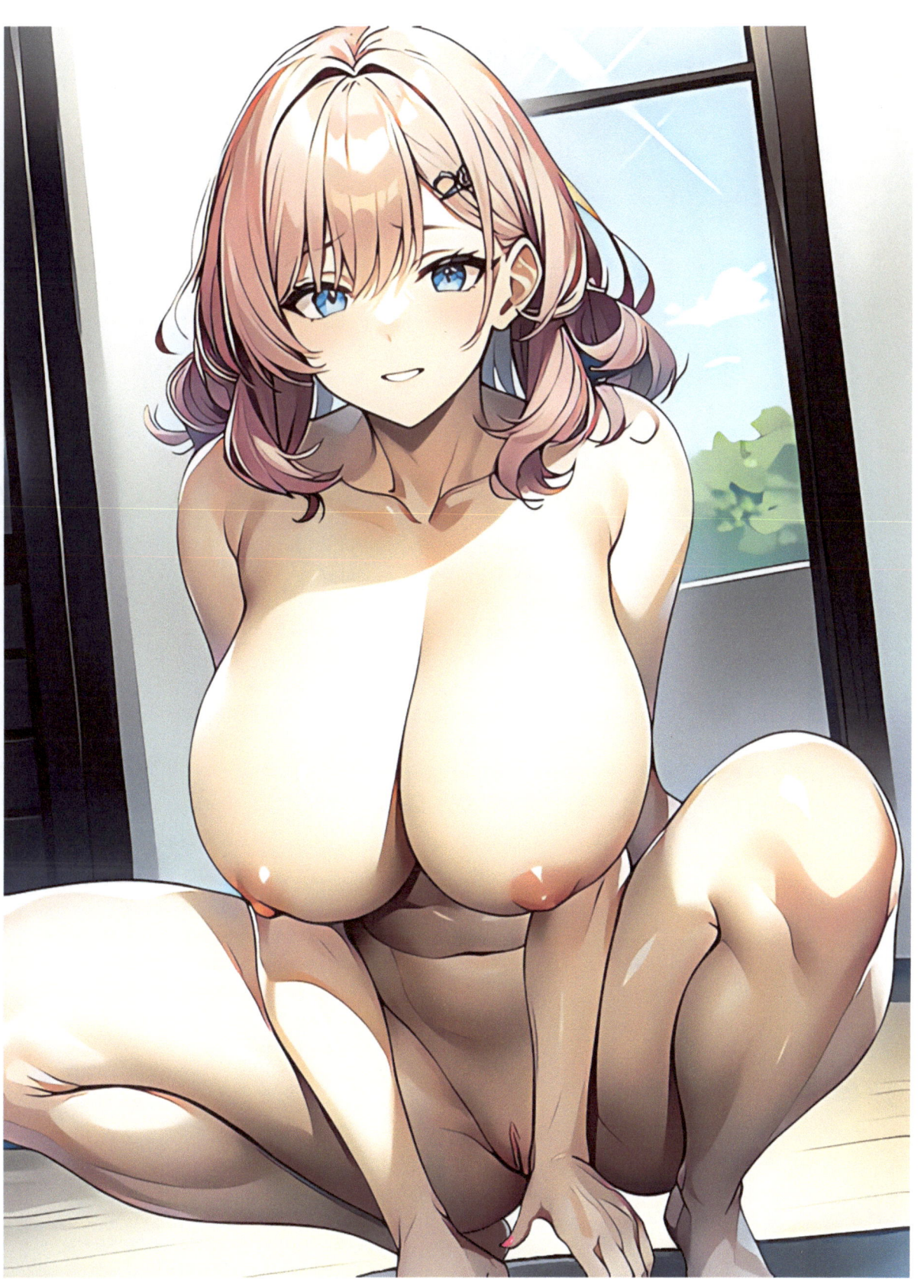

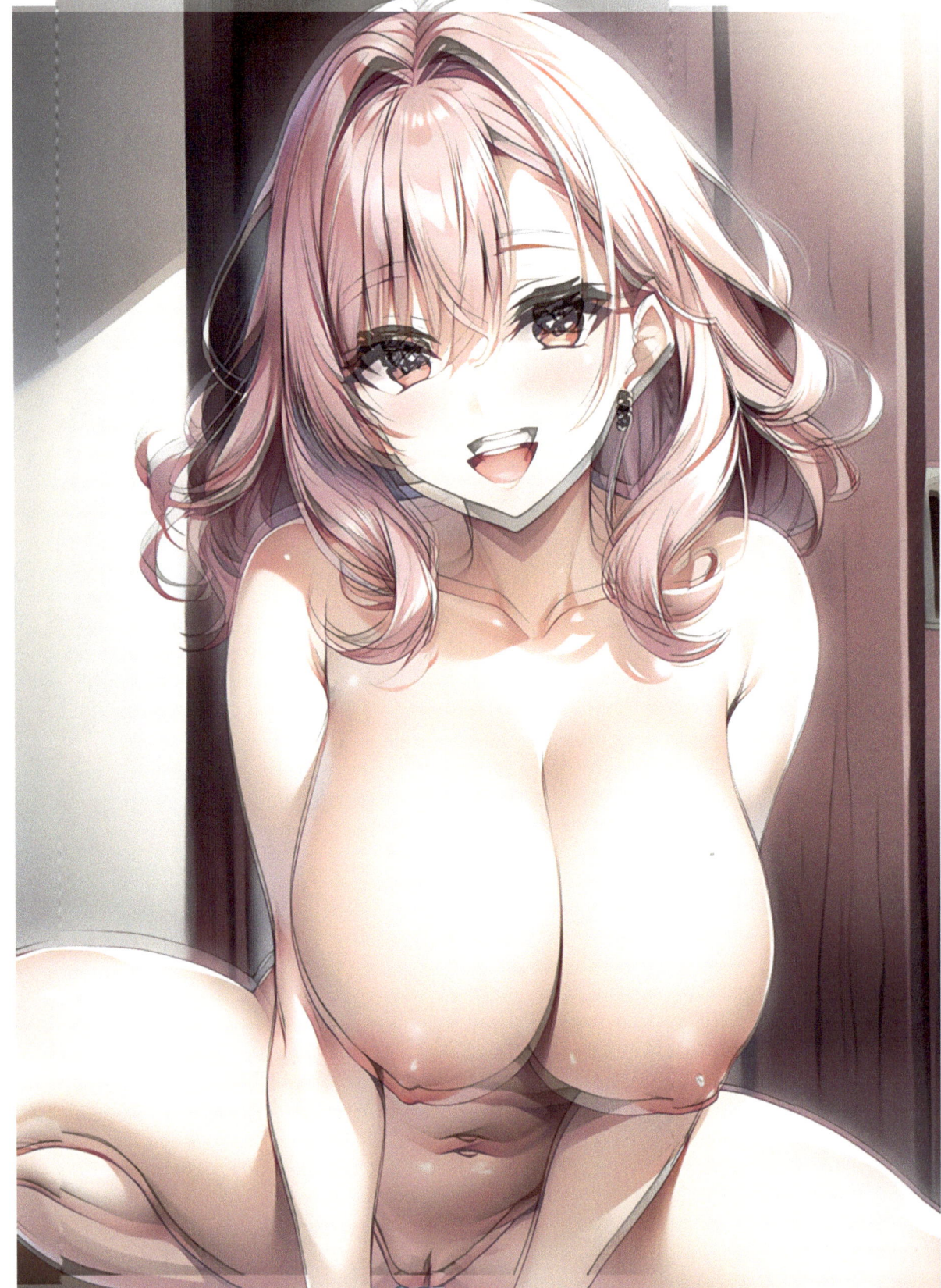

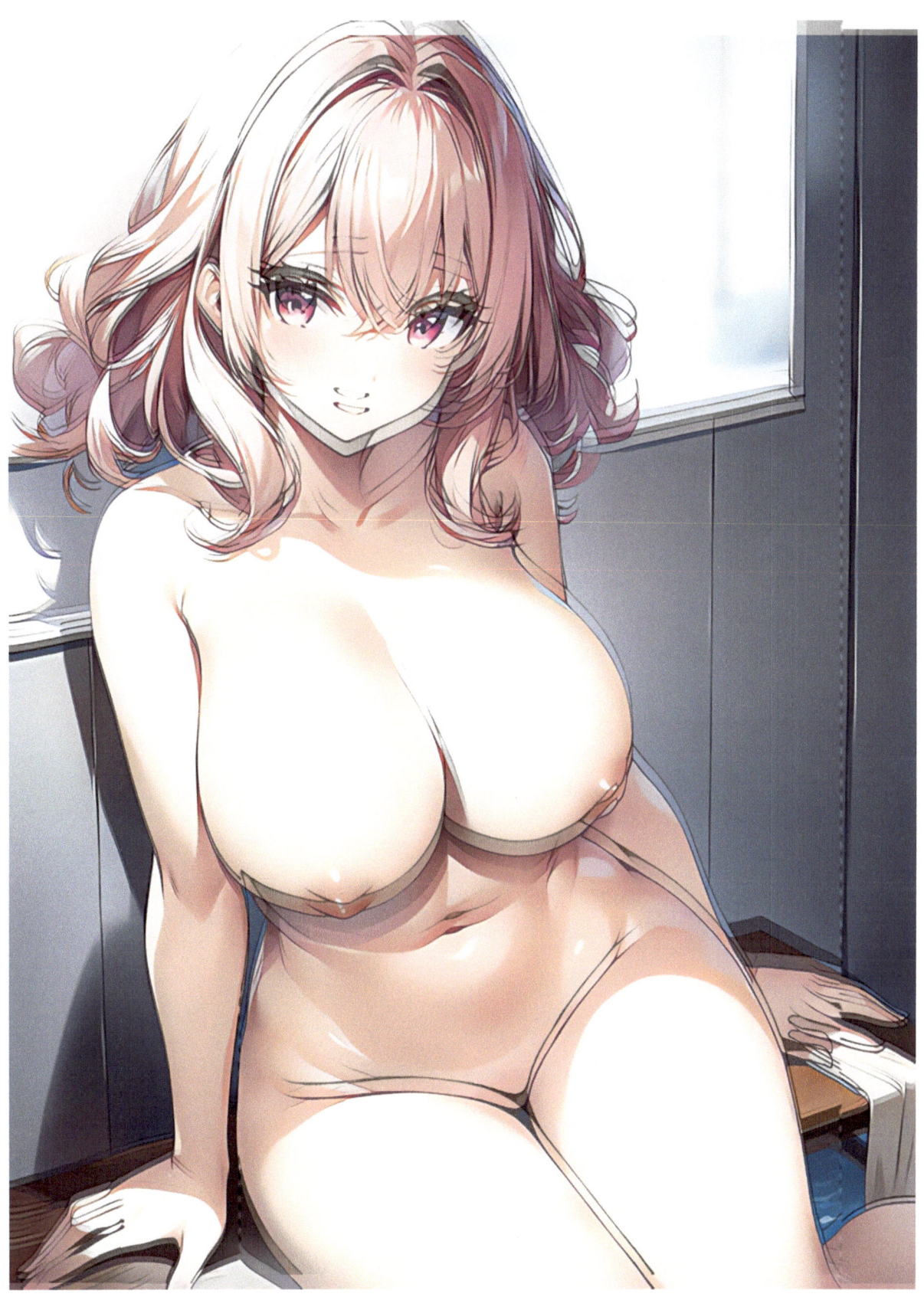

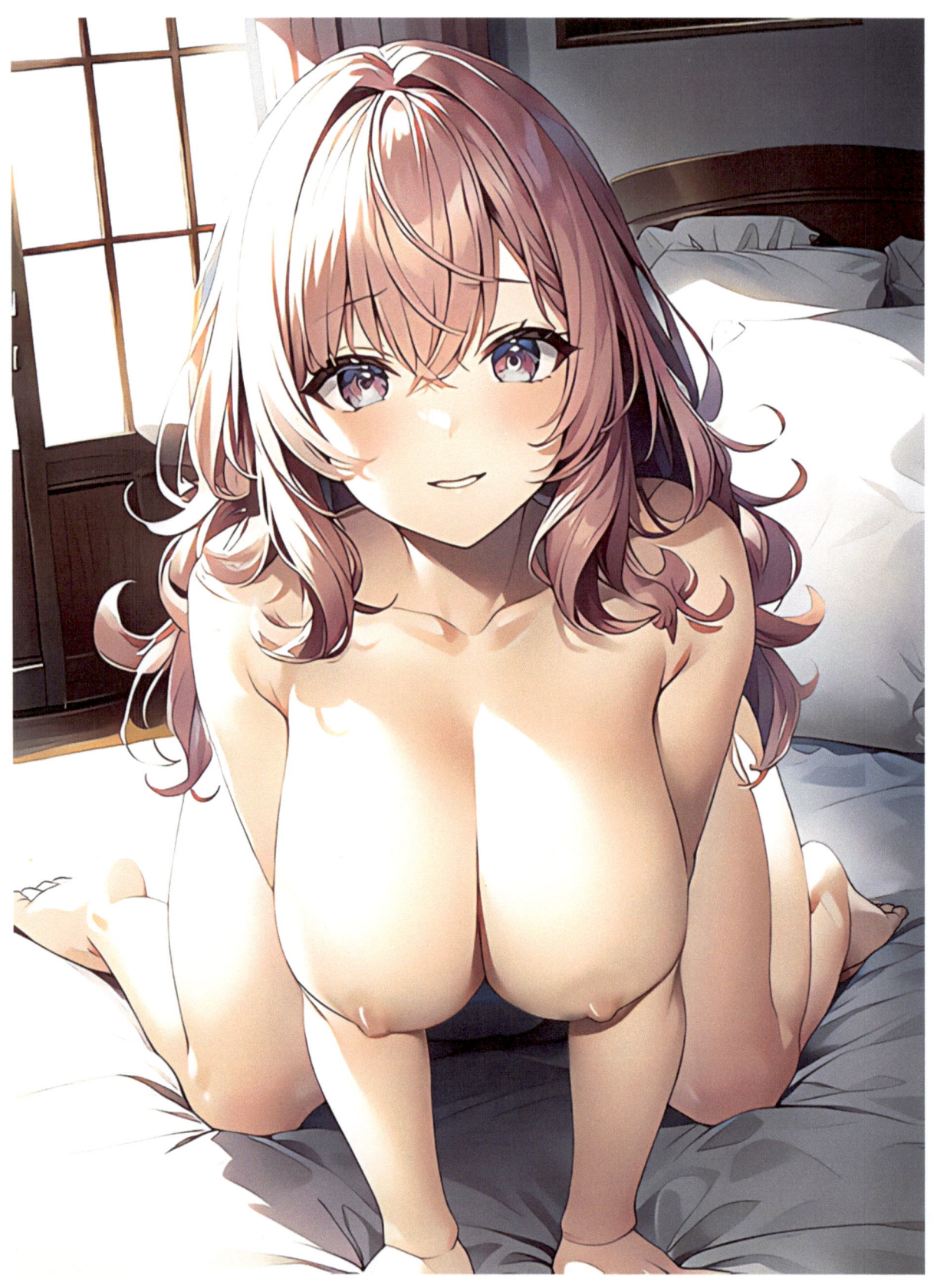

BOOK TITLE:

ACG TYPE PORTRAIT

PINKY GIRL

BY ZA STUDIO

Restrict-18.
Characters in the book are all adults.

www.ingramcontent.com/pod-product-compliance
Lightning Source LLC
Chambersburg PA
CBHW051924210526

45473CB00006B/2124